Our Living Constitution
Then and Now

Grades 5-8

by
Jerry Aten

Good Apple
An imprint of Carson-Dellosa Publishing LLC
Greensboro, North Carolina

Author: Jerry Aten
Editors: Kathleen Hex, Todd Sharp
Cover Artist: Natalie Moromisato
Interior Artist: Robert Greisen

Good Apple
An imprint of Carson-Dellosa Publishing LLC
PO Box 35665
Greensboro, NC 27425 USA

ISBN 978-0-7682-2456-6
01-181118091

Table of Contents

Introduction iv

Prelude to Independence 1–2

Declaration of Independence 3–10
    Activities 11–14

The Road to Change 15–20
    Activities 21–27

Article 1 – Legislative Department 28–33
    Sections 1–6, Activities 34–40

Article 1, Section 7 (Bills) 41–42
    Activities 43–46

Express Powers of Congress
    Article 1, Section 8 47–49
    Activities 50–52

Prohibitions on Congress/the States
    Article 1, Sections 9–10 53–55
    Activity 56

Article 2 – Executive Department
    Section 1 57–60
    Activities 61–68

Article 2 – Executive Department
    Sections 2–4 69–71
    Activity 72

Article 3 – Judicial Department 73–76
    Activities 77–80

Checks and Balances 81
    Activities 82–84

Article 4 – The States and the Federal Government 85–86
    Activity 87

Article 5 – Amending the Constitution 88
    Activity 89

Article 6 – General Provisions 90
    Activity 91

Article 7 – Ratification 92
    Activity 93

Review Articles 4–7 (Activity) 94
    Bill of Rights (Amendments 1–10) 95–101
    Activities 102–108

Amendments 11–12 109–111
    The Birth of Political Parties 112
    Activities 113–114

Election Day 115
    Activity 116

Amendments 13–15, The End of Slavery 117–120
    Activities 121–122

Amendment 16, Income Tax 123

Amendment 17, Direct Election of Senators 124

Amendment 18, Prohibition 125
    Activity 126

Amendment 19, Woman Suffrage 127
    Activity 128

Amendment 20, Lame Duck Amendment 129–130
    Activity 131

Amendment 21, The Repeal of Prohibition 132
    Activity 133

Amendment 22, President's Term of Office 134
    Activity 135

Amendment 23, The District of Columbia 136

Amendment 24, Poll Tax Abolished 137

Amendment 25, Presidential Disability
and Succession 138–139
    Activity 140

Amendment 26, Voting Age 141

Amendment 27, Pay Raises for Members
    of Congress 142

Our Amendments at Work (Activity) 143–145

Reviewing the Constitution (Activity) 146–148

We the People (Game) 149–160

Answer Key 161–171

Introduction

The Constitution of the United States is perhaps the single most imitated political document in the world. It has survived as our blueprint of government for more than 200 years. No other document anywhere can claim such enduring credentials. It is so important that most school systems include it as a part of the curriculum. But teaching the Constitution as it was written is no easy matter. It is a complex document written in legalistic language that makes it difficult for children to understand. The whole purpose of this book is to make passing on its rich and timeless message a little easier and more meaningful to the next generation.

The design of the lessons begins with a word of introduction and explanation. This is followed by a two-column layout. The paragraph, clause or section of the Constitution as it was written appears in the left column; an explanation in language students will understand is found in the column on the right. At the end of each lesson are discussion and thought-provoking questions that relate to the material just presented. The research activities shown with this symbol ⭐ will add even more enrichment to the experience of the material just presented. The lessons vary in length—some taking less than a class period to cover, while others require as much as three class periods plus outside work.

To put things into proper historical perspective, the book begins with a study of the Declaration of Independence. When students become aware of the difficulty the colonies had in gaining their freedom, they will have a greater appreciation of the Constitution. They will see how Shays' Rebellion clearly showed dissatisfaction among the people and how the Articles of Confederation just did not work as a framework of government. They will see how change became necessary and how the Constitution evolved through the cooperation and compromise of some highly intelligent and very determined statesmen. Finally, they will draw conclusions on why and how this precious document of ours has survived for over 200 years with only a few changes. One of the main focuses of the book is to show them how the Constitution relates to our lives today and how it serves us in the society in which we live.

When the entire study of the Constitution has been completed, the exciting game *We the People* can be used to provide a comprehensive review for a final examination. There are forty game cards, each containing four questions. The correct answers are on the backs of the cards. The format allows for the game's use by the entire class or as a competition between students working in pairs. A complete answer key containing suggested responses to all the questions is also included.

The Constitution as a separate unit can be studied any time during the year, but perhaps it becomes most meaningful to students when presented in its proper chronological segments of time in the story of America.

With proper background on how the Constitution evolved, students will clearly see the cause for many of its passages. Studying the Constitution will also help them to gain a more meaningful grasp of the changes that have occurred since the birth of our nation, to better appreciate their country's heritage, and to more deeply understand the rights and responsibilities they possess as American citizens.

Prelude to Independence

Although the Declaration of Independence and the U.S. Constitution were written for different purposes and under different conditions, the two documents have certain common grounds and ties together. The Declaration is for the most part a list of the reasons the colonists decided to break away from England. The fact that this declaration was made, however, did not make the colonists necessarily free.

With Lexington and its aftermath still ringing in their ears, the delegates of the Continental Congress began taking bold strides toward independence even though many still felt there could be ways to patch up their differences with England. Finally, on June 7, 1776, Richard Henry Lee of Virginia rose before the delegates and proposed his famous motion "That these United Colonies are, and of right ought to be, free and independent States. . . ." His motion was seconded by John Adams of Massachusetts, but final voting did not occur until July 2, when the Congress voted in favor of independence.

A committee was appointed to write a declaration of independence explaining to the world the reasons for the colonies taking such a drastic step. That committee was composed of John Adams, Benjamin Franklin, Robert Livingston, Roger Sherman, and Thomas Jefferson.

The committee turned to Jefferson to refine their ideas into a final document. No better choice could have been made. At the age of thirty-three, Jefferson was already recognized for his brilliance as an inventor and statesman. Although he wasn't a very good public speaker, he wrote extremely well. When he had finished, he had no idea that what he had composed would be regarded historically as one of the most beautifully written documents of all time.

His work was adopted on July 4,1776, by Congress. A white-wigged gentleman solemnly read the words to an anxious Philadelphia crowd. When he was finished, the people cheered and bells rang out all over the city. The colonists were aware of the grim task that lay before them. But they were convinced that the risks were worth the chance to be free from the harsh rule of the British crown. They knew they would have to earn their independence through the long and bitter struggle of the Revolutionary War.

Once the fight was won, it was time to set forth the principles that would run the new government. The intent was to lay down some rules that would give them enough control to prevent the government from infringing on their lives as King George had done. Their plan—the Articles of Confederation—did not work. It placed so many restrictions on the central government that there was no strength in its framework. That document was eventually replaced by the Constitution, a masterpiece of government that has survived more than 200 years. As you prepare to study the Constitution, it is helpful to take a look first at the Declaration of Independence. You will see how the complaints registered in the Declaration were answered and presented for future generations as they were dealt with in the Constitution.

As you read the following pages, you will find the original words of the Declaration of Independence in the left-hand column. After reading a paragraph from this side, read the paragraph in the right-hand column to get a more easily understood explanation. Also become aware as you read the five separate parts of the Declaration, that each serves a specific purpose. As you analyze the timeless passages of this document, make note of the specific purpose served by each of these parts: Preamble, statement of basic human rights, charges against the king and Parliament, statement of separation, signatures. Headings have been provided to show you the separation between the parts.

Declaration of Independence

In Congress, July 4, 1776. The unanimous Declaration of the thirteen united States of America,

When in the Course of human events, it becomes necessary for one people to dissolve the political bands which have connected them with another, and to assume among the powers of the earth, the separate and equal station to which the Laws of Nature and of Nature's God entitle them, a decent respect to the opinions of mankind requires that they should declare the causes which impel them to the separation.

We hold these truths to be self-evident, that all men are created equal, that they are endowed by their Creator with certain unalienable Rights, that among these are Life, Liberty, and the pursuit of Happiness.

That to secure these rights, Governments are instituted among Men, deriving their just powers from the consent of the governed,

Preamble

All thirteen states of America were in agreement to making this declaration on July 4, 1776.

Whenever it becomes necessary for one nation or group of people to declare itself free from the rule of another, then a common decency to the opinions of all other people requires that an explanation of the reasons for the declaration be made.

Statement of Human Rights

We believe these truths to be so obvious that they need no proof: That all people are created equal; that God gives all of us certain rights that cannot be taken away; that among these rights are life, liberty, and the freedom to find happiness.

To make certain these rights are protected and preserved for the people, governments are created. Those governments get this source of power from the people.

That whenever any Form of Government becomes destructive of these ends, it is the Right of the People to alter or to abolish it, and to institute new Government, laying its foundation on such principles and organizing its powers in such form, as to them shall seem most likely to effect their Safety and Happiness. Prudence, indeed, will dictate that Governments long established should not be changed for light and transient causes; and accordingly all experience hath shewn, that mankind are more disposed to suffer, while evils are sufferable, than to right themselves by abolishing the forms to which they are accustomed. But when a long train of abuses and usurpations, pursuing invariably the same Object evinces a design to reduce them under absolute Despotism, it is their right, it is their duty, to throw off such Government, and to provide new Guards for their future security.

If a government abuses this power, then the people have a right to change their government or get rid of it completely and start a new government that will better suit their needs. Common sense would tell us that an established government should not be overthrown for minor reasons. It is the nature of man to tolerate mistreatment rather than get rid of something he is used to and start a new government. But sometimes a government will go too far in abusing the rights of the people.

When this happens, it is not only the people's right, but their duty to overthrow the current government and set up a new government that will better protect their precious personal rights.

Such has been the patient sufferance of these Colonies; and such is now the necessity which constrains them to alter their former Systems of Government. The history of the present King of Great Britain is a history of repeated injuries and usurpations, all having in direct object the establishment of an absolute Tyranny over these States. To prove this, let Facts be submitted to a candid world.

Such has been the case thus far with the thirteen colonies. They have suffered patiently. But they now are convinced that they must change their government and must no longer accept the rule of King George III of England. He has a history of bad rule that abused the rights of the colonists and placed them completely under his control. To prove this, let the facts of his record be presented to an unbiased world.

Charges Against King George and Parliament

He has refused his Assent to Laws, the most wholesome and necessary for the public good.

He has refused to pass laws necessary for the good of the people.

He has forbidden his Governors to pass Laws of immediate and pressing importance, unless suspended in their operation till his Assent should be obtained; and when so suspended, he has utterly neglected to attend to them.

He has prevented those assigned to act as governors of the colonies from enforcing laws until he has approved them; and then he has neglected his duty to approve those laws.

He has refused to pass other Laws for the accommodation of large districts of people, unless those people would relinquish the right of Representation in the Legislature, a right inestimable to them and formidable to tyrants only.

He has refused to approve of laws needed to govern large groups of people unless these people are willing to give up their right to be represented in the legislature. This right is valuable to them and presents a threat to no one but a tyrant like himself.

He has called together legislative bodies at places unusual, uncomfortable, and distant from the depository of their public Records, for the sole purpose of fatiguing them into compliance with his measures.

He has called meetings of the legislature together in unusual places that are inconvenient to get to and often far distant from access to public records. His purpose in doing so has been to tire the legislators and make them more agreeable to the laws he wants passed.

He has dissolved Representative Houses repeatedly, for opposing with manly firmness his invasions on the rights of the people.

He has suspended those colonial legislatures that have dared to defy his rule by opposing laws he wanted passed—laws that were obvious invasions on the rights of people.

He has refused for a long time, after such dissolutions, to cause others to be elected; whereby the Legislative powers, incapable of Annihilation, have returned to the People at large for their exercise; the State remaining in the mean time exposed to all the dangers of invasion from without, and convulsions within.

Once those legislatures were dissolved, he refused to allow new legislators to be elected. As a result of this, the power to make laws, which cannot be destroyed, has returned to the people. That society without proper leadership is vulnerable to attack by outsiders and leaves a state of lawlessness and rebellion within.

He has endeavoured to prevent the population of these States; for that purpose obstructing the Laws for Naturalization of Foreigners; refusing to pass others to encourage their migrations hither, and raising the conditions of new Appropriations of Lands.

He has tried to prevent expansion from within the colonies in a number of ways: he has made difficult the naturalization of foreigners; he has refused to pass laws that would make immigration here more appealing; he has changed the conditions for acquiring new lands.

He has obstructed the Administration of Justice, by refusing his Assent to Laws for establishing Judiciary powers.

He has made it increasingly difficult for justice to prevail by refusing to approve of laws that would give power to the courts.

He has made Judges dependent on his Will alone, for the tenure of their offices, and the amount and payment of their salaries.

He has placed political pressure on judges by making their jobs and salaries solely dependent on their interpreting the laws through his wishes.

He has erected a multitude of New Offices, and sent hither swarms of Officers to harass our people, and eat out their substance.

He has created many new positions in government, then filled them with his own people who are sent among the colonists to harass them. And through all this, the people are still expected to pay the higher taxes that will support the salaries of these government workers.

He has kept among us, in times of peace, Standing Armies without the Consent of our legislatures.

He has kept standing armies of soldiers among us during times of peace without the approval of the legislature.

He has affected to render the Military independent of and superior to the Civil power.

He has tried to make the military independent of and superior to the civilian power of the people.

He has combined with others to subject us to a jurisdiction foreign to our constitution, and unacknowledged by our laws; giving his Assent to their Acts of pretended Legislation:

He has also committed several injustices to the people while working with Parliament. The result is a government in which the people have no voice. He has approved of those laws made by Parliament, but those laws are of no value to the colonists because they were made without the people having any voice in their creation. Here are some of the injustices done by Parliament and King George III.

For quartering large bodies of armed troops among us:

They have forced us to keep armed soldiers in our homes.

For protecting them, by a mock Trial, from punishment for any Murders which they should commit on the Inhabitants of these States:

They have protected those soldiers from punishment through a mock trial even when they committed murders against the inhabitants. (The specific reference to this charge is the phony trial that resulted from the Boston Massacre.)

For cutting off our Trade with all parts of the world:

They have stopped us from trading with many other countries by forcing us to trade only with England.

For imposing Taxes on us without our Consent:

They have levied taxes against us without our consent.

For depriving us in many cases, of the benefits of Trial by Jury:

They have on many occasions deprived us of the right to trial by jury.

For transporting us beyond Seas to be tried for pretended offenses:

They have transported some of our people all the way back to England to face charges that were trumped up to find ways to deal with those who have caused them trouble.

For abolishing the free System of English Laws in a neighbouring Province, establishing therein an Arbitrary government, and enlarging its Boundaries so as to render it at once an example and fit instrument for introducing the same absolute rule into these Colonies:

They abolished the free system of English Law in the Canadian province of Quebec, giving them instead a system of bad laws at the same time they enlarged that province. They have made it appear that they intend to impose the same type of bad rule in these colonies.

For taking away our Charters, abolishing our most valuable laws, and altering fundamentally the Forms of our Governments:

They have taken away our charters, abolishing our most precious and important laws. Without such laws, the governments are changed considerably.

For suspending our own Legislatures, and declaring themselves invested with power to legislate for us in all cases whatsoever.

They have kept our legislatures from meeting, declaring themselves as the lawmaking body with the power to make our laws for us.

He has abdicated Government here, by declaring us out of his Protection and waging War against us.

The King has given up his power to govern us, because he has refused to protect us and has waged war against us.

He has plundered our seas, ravaged our Coasts, burnt our towns, and destroyed the lives of our people.

He has attacked our ships and coastlines and has burned our towns and "destroyed" the ability of the people to make lives for themselves.

He is at this time transporting large Armies of foreign Mercenaries to compleat the works of death, desolation and tyranny, already begun with circumstances of Cruelty & perfidy scarcely paralleled in the most barbarous ages, and totally unworthy the Head of a civilized nation.

He has hired large armies of mercenary soldiers to come here to fight against us and continue his works of treachery. His cruel and barbaric acts make him totally unworthy of his title and unfit to rule a civilized nation.

He has constrained our fellow Citizens taken Captive on the high Seas to bear Arms against their Country, to become the executioners of their friends and Brethren, or to fall themselves by their Hands.

He has forced our fellow Americans whom he has captured on the high seas to fight against other Americans.

He has excited domestic insurrections amongst us, and has endeavoured to bring on the inhabitants of our frontiers, the merciless Indian Savages, whose known rule of warfare, is an undistinguished destruction of all ages, sexes and conditions.

He has incited some of the colonists to rebel against their own colonial governments. He has aroused the Indians on our borders to complete savage attacks against our people.

In every stage of these Oppressions We have Petitioned for Redress in the most humble terms: Our repeated Petitions have been answered only by repeated injury. A Prince, whose character is thus marked by every act which may define a Tyrant, is unfit to be the ruler of a free people.

During the entire period of these injustices, we begged him to listen in the most humble of terms. Every plea was only met with another injury. From this action it is quite obvious that this king is a tyrant and unfit to rule a free people.

Nor have We been wanting in attentions to our Brittish brethren. We have warned them from time to time of attempts by their legislature to extend an unwarrantable jurisdiction over us.

We have appealed to our British brethren. We have warned them from time to time about how we feel about the rule of Parliament and the King.

We have reminded them of the circumstances of our emigration and settlement here.

We have reminded them that we are still their kin who came here in search of a new chance and better life.

We have appealed to their native justice and magnanimity, and we have conjured them by the ties of our common kindred to disavow these usurpations, which, would inevitably interrupt our connections and correspondence. They too have been deaf to the voice of justice and of consanguinity.

We have appealed to their common sense and compassion to do what is naturally right. We have called on their sense of common ties with us, telling them that a continuation of these actions would result in our breaking our common bond with them. Our words have fallen on deaf ears.

We must, therefore, acquiesce in the necessity, which denounces our Separation, and hold them, as we hold the rest of mankind, Enemies in War, in Peace Friends.

We must therefore announce our separation from them and regard as we do the rest of mankind—enemies in war, friends in peace.

We, therefore, the Representatives of the united States of America, in General Congress, Assembled, appealing to the Supreme Judge of the world for the rectitude of our intentions, do, in the Name, and by Authority of the good People of these Colonies, solemnly publish and declare, That these United Colonies are, and of Right ought to be Free and Independent States; that they are Absolved from all Allegiance to the British Crown, and that all political connection between them and the State of Great Britain, is and ought to be totally dissolved;

and that as Free and Independent States, they have full Power to levy War, conclude Peace, contract Alliances, establish Commerce, and to do all other Acts and Things which Independent States may of right do.

And for the support of this Declaration, with a firm reliance on the protection of divine Providence, we mutually pledge to each other our Lives, our Fortunes and our sacred Honor.

Statement of Separation

Therefore as the representatives of the people meeting in this Congress, we appeal to God for approval of our actions. We thus solemnly declare that these united colonies are and of right ought to be free and independent states,

that they no longer owe any loyalty to the English King and that all political ties with Great Britain are totally dissolved.

That as free and independent states they have the power to wage war, make peace, make alliances with other nations, promote trade and do all the other things that free and independent states have the right to do.

And in full support of this Declaration, with a firm reliance on the protection of God, we mutually pledge to each other our lives, our destinies and our sacred honor.

Name_____

Tell in which part of the Declaration of Independence each of the following is located by matching the correct letter. If you are familiar with the purpose of each part of the Declaration, you won't even need to use your notes.

a. charges against King George
b. statement of basic human rights
c. Preamble
d. statement of separation
e. signer of the Declaration

1. _____ We hold these truths to be self-evident …

2. _____ …we mutually pledge to each other our Lives …

3. _____ He has plundered our seas, ravaged our Coasts …

4. _____ He has dissolved Representative Houses …

5. _____ … they should declare the causes which impel them to the separation.

6. _____ Prudence, indeed, will dictate that governments long established should not be changed for light and transient causes …

7. _____ … that these United Colonies are, and of Right ought to be, Free …

8. _____ He has kept among us, in times of peace, Standing Armies …

9. _____ John Hancock

10. _____ … for imposing Taxes upon us without our Consent.

11. _____ A Prince, whose character is marked by every act which may define a Tyrant, is unfit to be the ruler of a free people.

12. _____ … to secure the rights, Governments are instituted among Men …

13. _____ When in the Course of human events …

14. _____ Charles Carroll of Carrollton

15. _____ He has excited domestic insurrections amongst us …

Name_____

We Hold These Truths

Choose from the list of words that are found in the Declaration of Independence the appropriate letters of the words that match the phrases in italics.

a. perfidy   f. endowed   k. endeavoured
b. harass   g. transient   l. evinces
c. convulsions   h. acquiesce   m. unwarrantable
d. annihilation   i. consanguinity   n. redress
e. mercenaries   j. prudence   o. magnanimity

1. _____ He has hired armies of *paid soldiers*.

2. _____ . . . the State remaining exposed to all dangers of invasion from without, and *violent disturbances* within.

3. _____ In every stage of these Oppressions We have Petitioned for *correction of these wrongs* in the most humble terms . . .

4. _____ *Common sense* indeed, will tell us that Governments long established will not be changed for light and transient causes . . .

5. _____ They too have been deaf to the voice of justice and of blood *relationship*.

6. _____ We have warned them from time to time of attempts . . . to extend an *unjustifiable* jurisdiction over us.

7. _____ He has erected a multitude of New Offices, and sent hither swarms of Officers to *persecute* our people . . .

8. _____ He has excited domestic insurrections amongst us, and has *tried* to bring on the inhabitants of our frontier . . .

9. _____ . . . that all men are created equal, that they are *blessed with* by their Creator with certain unalienable Rights . . .

10. _____ . . . the Legislative powers, incapable of *being destroyed* . . .

11. _____ We must, therefore, *agree* in the necessity which denounces our separation.

12. _____ We have appealed to their native justice and *courageous spirit* . . .

13. _____ But when a long train of abuses . . . *clearly shows* a design to reduce them . . .

14. _____ He is . . . transporting large Armies of foreign Mercenaries to compleat the works . . . of Cruelty and *treachery scarcely unparalleled* . . .

15. _____ Prudence . . . will dictate that governments long established should not be changed for light and *trifling* causes . . .

Our Basic Human Rights

1. According to Thomas Jefferson, what were the three basic human rights to which all of us are entitled by the mere fact that we exist?

_____

_____

_____

2. Why did Thomas Jefferson end up drafting the entire Declaration by himself, when a committee of five had been assigned the job?

_____

_____

_____

_____

_____

_____

3. According to the words of Thomas Jefferson, when do the people of a nation have the right to change their government by abandoning a system they do not like?

_____

_____

_____

4. From where do governments derive their power to make the laws that govern people?

_____

_____

5. Do you agree with Jefferson's statement that all men are created equal? Develop an explanatory paragraph of your thoughts with justification for your answer.

_____

_____

_____

_____

_____

6. Benjamin Franklin remarked at the signing of the Declaration that " . . . we must indeed all hang together, or assuredly, we shall all hang separately." What did Franklin mean by this statement?

_____

_____

_____

7. The name of John Hancock is the first to appear among the signers of the Declaration. His name has become so famous as a result that it is often used synonymously with the term *signature*. Research the circumstances surrounding Hancock's bold signature and tell how the word *signature* is associated with his name.

_____

_____

_____

The Road to Change

During the Revolution, the small farmer prospered. The British, the French, and the American armies all needed food and were willing to pay dearly for it. But when the war ended and the foreign armies went home, the demand for crops dropped dramatically. In 1786, farmers in Massachusetts became enraged over low farm prices. The Revolution had been won, and with it came independence. But prosperity was far down the road for these poor farmers who owed huge amounts of money. They had no chance to pay off their debts because the state taxes they had to pay were high—yet the price they received for their crops was very low. Creditors began to seize their farms. They pleaded with the government for help, but none came.

Hundreds of angry farmers and veterans, led by Daniel Shays, took the matter into their own hands. They attempted to capture a U.S. arsenal but were beaten back by the Massachusetts Militia. Historically, the incident is known as Shays' Rebellion, but the implications of why it happened are far more important than the incident itself. As we examine the reasons for disagreement in the new nation, you will see why it became necessary to change the entire framework of the national government and that the attempt to change it is what led to the Constitution, which has served us well for more than 200 years.

When the thirteen colonies had lived under English rule, they had functioned much as though they were thirteen separate little countries. Each had been established for economic or religious reasons all its own, and there was no real reason for them to unite in a common cause. The mistreatment they had experienced from King George was the cause that finally banded them together in their fight to be free. But once that fight was won and the war had ended, it was difficult for each to think of giving up its own special interests for the sake of a national government. The states pretty much went back to functioning as though they were thirteen separate nations. And that is where the problems began.

The Continental Congress had created the Articles of Confederation during the war to loosely tie the colonies together. Each state sent delegates, but the delegates had no real power. Every time an important vote came up, the delegates had to contact their individual states to find out how they should vote. No state was willing to give up its power for the sake of a strong central government. Finally, in 1781, the states agreed to a loose association that gave up only a few of their powers to the federal government, but they kept the most important powers for their own separate states. Such an arrangement is referred to as a *confederation,* and the document was called the *Articles of Confederation and Perpetual Union.*

The Confederation had no president nor were there any United States courts. The only branch of government was the Congress and it contained only one house. Each state voted as a single unit, but larger states did have more representatives than smaller states. Some of the powers the Congress had were to declare war, to receive foreign diplomats, to raise an army and navy, to control Indian affairs, to borrow money, to establish post offices, and to fix standards of weights and measures.

But there were many other important powers which Congress did not have. Congress had no power to regulate trade among the states. Each state had its own trade laws and the tariff each imposed on others was often so high that trade was discouraged. Congress had no power to enforce the laws it did make. If the states didn't accept a law, they simply disobeyed it. Congress could not levy taxes. Therefore it could not pay the debts of the United States nor provide the goods and services a central government should provide for its people. Congress could not prevent the individual states from issuing their own money. This obviously presented a number of problems in exchange and value and further discouraged trade and travel among people in the various

states. Congress had no power to defend any of the states separately or provide them with aid; nor could it act directly against individuals or states.

When comparing what Congress could do with what it could not do, it's quite obvious that the states were unwilling to give up any of their important powers to the central government under the Articles of Confederation. And that is the whole reason why that kind of government failed. The self-serving interests of the various states prevented them from acting other than as thirteen separate nations, and the United States was fast losing its credibility as a nation with the rest of the world.

With each passing year, the situation grew worse. Trade wars, boundary disputes and unrest among these people living in the United States caused many leaders to recognize a need for a stronger central government. George Washington took the initiative by inviting officials from Virginia and Maryland to his home at Mount Vernon to decide a way to settle a dispute between the two states over the use of the Potomac River.

The results brought about a second meeting at Annapolis, Maryland, in 1786, in which several other states sent representatives to talk about the trade and boundary problems generated by the philosophy of the Articles of Confederation. From that meeting came the call for a special convention to meet in Philadelphia in 1787 to revise the Articles of Confederation.

That convention gathered in May of 1787. There were representatives from all of the states except Rhode Island. Rhode Island refused to send any delegates because it feared the Convention would remove its power to tax the goods that passed through the state. The fifty-five who were there were indeed a distinguished body of political leaders. They were men of remarkable ability and had been carefully chosen by the states they represented.

The Convention promptly chose George Washington as president of the Convention. James Madison took copious notes for everything that was said and done at the Convention and became history's main source of information. There were also such distinguished men of the day as Benjamin Franklin, Alexander Hamilton, Roger Sherman, William Paterson and Gouverneur Morris (who actually put the document into its final form once all decisions had been made). As a group they were fairly young. Most of them were under the age of fifty. They were well-educated and represented several walks of life. There

were lawyers and businessmen and southern plantation owners. Some had been members of the Confederation Congress. All of them had spent a part of their lives in service to the public. All of them represented backgrounds of at least moderate financial success.

Once the delegates began their discussions, they quickly realized that no amount of correcting the Articles of Confederation would give them the strong framework of central government the nation sorely needed. Thus, they decided to start all over and write an entirely new plan that would replace the Articles of Confederation. They also decided to work behind closed doors, preferring to wait until the entire Constitution was written—then to submit the entire document to the states and the people for their approval.

Their first major decision was to establish three branches of government: the legislative branch to make the laws, the executive branch to enforce them, and the judicial branch to interpret the laws and try those accused of breaking them. They also agreed that a strong central government should be able to do almost all the things that the Articles of Confederation had not allowed. The delegates felt they should establish a *federal system* in which the power would be divided between the states and the central government.

But there were many areas of disagreement among the chosen delegates, some of which almost led to the Convention's dissolution. Each delegate was representing the best interests of his own state; and because the states had functioned much as separate nations, there were many areas where their values and goals would collide.

One major area of disagreement lay in the matter of how representation in the legislature would be figured. The larger states felt that a state's number of representatives should be determined by population. Their plan was proposed by Edmund Randolph of Virginia and

was called the Virginia Plan. On the other side of the aisle were the states with fewer people who feared that the big states would control the government, so they insisted that all states have equal representation. Their plan was the idea of William Paterson and was called the New Jersey Plan. The conflict over which of these proposals would be adopted threatened to break up the Convention. Roger Sherman of Connecticut came forth at the point of disaster with a compromise that appeased both the larger states and the smaller states. His proposal called for a two-house legislature. There would be an upper house called the Senate in which each state would have equal representation. There would also be a lower house, the House of Representatives, in which each state would have one representative for every 30,000 inhabitants living in that state. Sherman's plan satisfied both the smaller states and the more populous states. It became historically known as the Connecticut Compromise or the Great Compromise.

Another area of great controversy lay in the manner of determining taxes. Taxes were to be based on the number of people in each state.

For example, a larger state with twice as many people as a smaller state had to pay twice as much in taxes to support the national government. People living in the southern states did not want their slaves counted in the population because it would make their taxes higher as a result. They considered their slaves as property. But representation in the House of Representatives was based on population and the southern states wanted their slaves counted when it came to determining the number of representatives they would have. The delegates from the northern states felt just the opposite. Again the framers of the Constitution appeared to have reached a standoff with neither side willing to change its position.

Again compromise was the order of the day with a proposal brought forth called a *federal ratio* to solve the problem. In effect the proposal called for states to count three of every five slaves in their population, both for purposes of determining representation and taxation. The measure became known as the *three-fifths compromise.* The authors of the Constitution also carefully avoided using the word *slave* in the Constitution, but the issue constantly emerged because of the different economic concerns and values between the northern states and the southern slaveholding states.

On the issue of whether or not to allow slave trading, they finally settled the issue by allowing it to continue for twenty years through 1807—no doubt hoping that the issue would resolve itself by that time.

Finally, the delegates wrestled with the problem of how much power to give to the central government. They knew it had to be strong, because the Articles of Confederation had not provided for a strong central government and they had failed. But there needed to be some way to check and restrain the powers given to the central government to keep it from the potential abuses of unlimited powers. This they accomplished by having each of the three branches of government accountable to the other two. The Congress, for example, can make laws, but the President has the power to veto those he feels are not in the best interests of the nation. Congress can still override his veto, but the Supreme Court then has the power to rule out any law which they feel does not fall in line with the Constitution.

Because the delegates sent to the Convention didn't actually have the power to write a new Constitution, there was going to have to be approval from the states before it could become law. The Constitution itself provided for the rules of its ratification (Article 7). When the entire document was finished and signed, copies were dispatched to each of the states. Special conventions were then held in each of the states with the approval of nine states required to make the Constitution the law of the land. By the end of June in 1788, nine states had ratified the Constitution, but neither Virginia nor New York was among them. Everyone knew that without these two states the new Constitution would never work. Virginia and New York had not ratified the Constitution because many people in those states had objected to there not being much emphasis on individual rights in the new framework of government. Both states finally approved the Constitution with the condition that a number of amendments outlining specific rights and protection to individuals be added "at the earliest possible moment."

Congress did propose such a listing of human rights when it met in 1789 and by 1791 that list, known as the Bill of Rights, became a part of the Constitution.

Both North Carolina and Rhode Island eventually approved the Constitution, but not until the new government was already in operation.

The Background

1. What caused the historical incident referred to as "Shays' Rebellion"? Why was it a sign of the times?

   _____

   _____

   _____

   _____

   _____

   _____

2. The men who wrote the Constitution actually gathered together with the idea of merely revising the Articles of Confederation. They found the Articles to be so unworkable that they decided to start all over. List some of the more important reasons for the framers of the Constitution making the decision to write an entirely new framework of government.

   _____

   _____

   _____

   _____

   _____

   _____

   _____

   _____

   _____

3. One of the big questions faced by the Convention was the debate over the matter of representation in the Congress. Describe the controversy between the large states and the smaller states and the major provisions of the New Jersey and Virginia Plans. How was the issue finally resolved through compromise?

    Virginia Plan (large states): _____

    _____

    _____

    New Jersey Plan (small states): _____

    _____

    _____

    The Great Compromise: _____

    _____

    _____

4. Another compromise emerged over the matter of counting slaves. Explain how the southern views differed from those of the North and how the "three-fifths clause" saved the day.

    _____

    _____

    _____

    _____

    _____

    _____

    _____

    _____

5. It has been said that the Constitution is ". . . the most wonderful work ever struck off at a given time by the brain and purpose of man." How can such a statement be made about a document that has already been changed (amended) twenty-seven times?

_____

_____

_____

_____

_____

_____

6. Give examples from history or today that support this statement: "Those who control the power to govern are resistant to any kind of change because they fear such changes will decrease their power."

_____

_____

_____

_____

_____

7. Rhode Island was the only state not represented at the Constitutional Convention. Why did this tiny state refuse to send delegates to such an important and historical meeting?

_____

_____

_____

_____

_____

8. The delegates who came to the Constitutional Convention represented several different occupations. Among them were several lawyers, businessmen, and southern plantation owners. There were other occupations, but none of them were less than at least moderately successful financially. Why do you suppose none of the men were what could be called "common men"?

_____

_____

_____

_____

9. Soon after they convened, the delegates decided to work behind closed doors. Why do you think they made that decision?

_____

_____

_____

_____

10. When we think of the U.S. Constitution, we usually think of the name of George Washington. Even though he was very important as president of the Convention, there were several other names we should remember as well. Below are the names of several of these leaders who were at the Philadelphia Convention. Choose any two and research the contribution made by each; then write an essay describing the contribution of each as well as developing a contrast between the two.

Oliver Ellsworth	Rufus King	John Dickinson
Roger Sherman	John Rutledge	Alexander Hamilton
Robert Morris	William Samuel Johnson	Charles Pinckney
George Wythe	Gouverneur Morris	
James Madison	Benjamin Franklin	
William Paterson	Edmund Randolph	

Drawing Conclusions

Below are the results of the votes taken in each state by the special convention called to ratify the Constitution. Look closely at them and decide which of the conclusions can be called true and which cannot. Write *true* or *false* on the line before each statement.

State	Date	For Ratification	Against
1. Delaware	Dec. 7, 1787	30	0
2. Pennsylvania	Dec. 12, 1787	46	23
3. New Jersey	Dec. 18, 1787	38	0
4. Georgia	Jan. 2, 1788	26	0
5. Connecticut	Jan. 9, 1788	128	40
6. Massachusetts	Feb. 6, 1788	187	168
7. Maryland	Apr. 28, 1788	63	11
8. South Carolina	May 23, 1788	149	73
9. New Hampshire	June 21, 1788	57	47
10. Virginia	June 25, 1788	89	79
11. New York	July 26, 1788	30	27
12. North Carolina	Nov. 21, 1789	196	77
13. Rhode Island	May 29, 1790	34	32

1. _____ The closest vote was in the state of New York.

2. _____ Conventions in all 13 states approved ratification of the Constitution.

3. _____ The southern states were more favorable toward ratification than the New England states.

4. _____ The states which ratified the Constitution earliest seemed to do so with overwhelming approval.

5. _____ Connecticut had the widest margin of votes in favor of ratification.

6. _____ Pennsylvania delegates approved of the Constitution by a vote of 2:1.

7. _____ The Constitution went into effect before all states had approved its ratification.

8. _____ The state with the most delegates was North Carolina.

9. _____ Three states ratified the Constitution unanimously.

10. _____ The big states were more in favor of the Constitution than the small states.

Draw three conclusions of your own from the voting results in the chart above that are different from those already stated. Write your conclusions on the back of this paper.

 076822456X • Our Living Constitution

Preamble

The original Constitution contained seven articles. There have been twenty-seven changes or additions to those seven articles. The changes are called amendments. The very first paragraph that precedes the actual text of the Constitution is called the Preamble. It summarizes the reasons why the Constitution was written. We might better call the Preamble a *statement of purpose*.

We the people of the United States, in order to form a more perfect Union,	We the representatives of the American people; in order to make a better, more efficient system of government than was possible under the Articles of Confederation,
establish justice,	so that all people are treated fairly under the same laws,
insure domestic tranquility,	to ensure a peaceful existence within the United States,
provide for the common defense,	to ensure an adequate defense against those who would be our enemies,
promote the general welfare, and	to encourage what is good for all the people, and
secure the blessings of liberty to ourselves and our posterity,	to keep our freedom and make certain that our children and our children's children have those same freedoms,
do ordain and establish this Constitution for the United States of America.	create and issue this Constitution for our nation.

Summarize in a paragraph the reasons why the Constitution was written.

_____

_____

_____

_____

_____

If a new Constitution were to be written today, what reasons, other than those cited in the Preamble, would you list as reasons for writing a constitution? Use the back of this page.

Preamble Scramble

Below is the Preamble to the Constitution of the United States. Your task is to find it in this jumble of letters. You may make only 90° turns, but you may move your pencil in any direction.

```
T W E T H E P E O P L E R V W I T E R P S R T O F D O M N U X Y M
O R M T H Z Q O P S O O I H M N T D S O K R A B C Z P E P F Q O R
E T I N U F O E H T F F T H E U O S T S O C P F E H R T O I R M V
P E R F E C T U S K T B A N R E L T A A B A K C A B F Y A N V A S
T E W O H A P N T M H A N A P U B A L S K O C D T U F B R E W Y M
R L T M T S M I A V E U N I T E D T U P N E I R F T S E B Y R E V
Q F S P Y B O O R O H L I T D O S E A T E S O F B E F R E I A N E
E S O S R U R N S I E A H W I N G S C O M E S A S T O T S A J R O
E R O M A M R O F O T R E D R O N I A C I R E M I H S I N E R G G
P R U S N I N N A T S E Z H T W Z I L A R O N M M E S T N I V R R
E R F E C T U L I S H J U S T I C E I N O N E O L T I C A T I S
E D O M E S N E B W O N T H Y B F L D N S U R E D G C C T O T U O
L V Q C I T I V A F D N O M Y A R O O V A P A B A G N T O M H E I
I I N A R T O V T L S O P O M O R G F O R R H L T S E R F E D I D
T Y A F D N N E S O Y D O T M A P T H O F F S I T R Y A N Q U I L
S R T N A Y S A I T S U P E P I E R E E O R T Y H E E A R S M A I
D E H O Y S T P S H T J E T E A S G N O M M O C E H T R O F D R T
A F L E W L A R E N E G E H N I N T D T E L H V S I T T R E N I Y
O A N C E M W E H I W M I H G T E F E N T B I A G N O S E D A O P
D R E H W I H N E R N T H E P O R L A D W T S D A D A T T I V O R
O E N V O I H T N A C H E L L P E D U H O I F Y A R P E Y F T Y H
U A N D H T E M N N G S O F O D D R N E K C I G D S R N I F A T E
T T V S S T I H T I N H I L B V T S E L V E S A N D A I T Y D O O
I J E E M T G P V S L H M I I T U R B T C M E N T O V R S I S A R
S U T C T H T U V S E T I B H H O U E T D U D H S U I E O N I T D
T J D U S V O P O E M H N E T G M O J R E L P R E R L T H T E C A
G E N R E T H E B L V M O R T Y T O V D A D N A R P O S E N R O I
E R A C O N S T I T U T I O N F O R T H H S I L B A T S E D N A N
E D L A R A S A C I V M O T S T I N V H T P V O A H E M A U T N E
F A N Y A S L G E L G I L O L M O S S O H I S C O N S T I T U T I
G R O A G T F O H O C N K D D O R F A F H T H O Y T N I C S D C O
N T U N D A C I R E M A F O S E T A T S D E T I N U E H T R O F N
C E I H A D F O T W E N T O S T O L L C C S T R I N G J S A T O U
```

Article I – Legislative Department

Article 1 clearly points out the powers and restrictions of the legislative or lawmaking branch of our government. Several changes have been made to Article 1 since it was written, but it is important to study the original text first to better understand why it was necessary for those changes.

Article I, Section 1. All legislative powers herein granted shall be vested in a Congress of the United States, which shall consist of a Senate and House of Representatives.

Power Defined

The power to make laws that govern the people of the United States is given to Congress. Congress is made up of two separate houses; one is called the U.S. Senate, the other is the House of Representatives.

Article I, Section 2, clause 1. The House of Representatives shall be composed of members chosen every second year by the people of the several states, and the electors in each state shall have the qualifications requisite for electors of the most numerous branch of the state legislature.

House of Representatives

Members of the House of Representatives are chosen by voters of the states they represent. Elections are held every two years. People who are allowed to vote for their own state lawmakers shall also be eligible to vote for the representatives of the House. *Many states formerly had restrictions on who could vote. Amendments to the Constitution have lifted those restrictions.*

Article I, Section 2, clause 2. No person shall be a representative who shall not have attained to the age of twenty-five years, and been seven years a citizen of the United States, and who shall not, when elected, be an inhabitant of that state in which he shall be chosen.

Qualifications

To become a member of the U.S. House of Representatives, one must:

1. be 25 years of age
2. be a U.S. citizen for at least seven years
3. live in the state from which he or she is chosen

Since the Constitution was written, most states have been divided into districts—each district being allowed one representative.

Article I, Section 2, clause 3.
Representatives and direct taxes shall be apportioned among the several states which may be included within this Union, according to their respective numbers, [which shall be determined by adding to the whole number of free persons, including those bound to service for a term of years, and excluding Indians not taxed, three-fifths of all other persons].

The actual enumeration shall be made within three years after the first meeting of the Congress of the United States, and within every subsequent term of ten years, in such manner as they shall by law direct.

The number of representatives shall not exceed one for every thirty thousand, but each state shall have at least one representative; [and until such enumeration shall be made, the state of New Hampshire shall be entitled to choose 3, Massachusetts 8, Rhode Island and Providence Plantations 1, Connecticut 5, New York 6, New Jersey 4, Pennsylvania 8, Delaware 1, Maryland 6, Virginia 10, North Carolina 5, South Carolina 5, and Georgia 3].

Article I, Section 2, clause 4. When vacancies happen in the representation from any state, the executive authority thereof shall issue writs of election to fill such vacancies.

Article I, Section 2, clause 5. The House of Representatives shall choose their Speaker and other officers;

Representation

The number of representatives each state is allowed is determined by the population of that state. *Two parts of this clause no longer apply. Direct taxes are no longer based on population, but rather income (16th Amendment). Also the 13th Amendment nullified the three-fifths clause because it outlawed slavery.*

A census or count of the people is authorized by Congress every ten years beginning with the first year of the decade.

The number of representatives for each state was originally based on 30,000 persons per representative. Because the population has grown a great deal, there are now many more than 30,000 persons represented by each representative. But the proportion remains the same. That is, each congressional district has about the same number of persons. In 1910, the number of representatives was frozen at 435.

Filling Vacancies

When a representative dies or resigns his or her office, the governor of the state he or she represents calls for a special election to fill the vacancy.

Organization

The House of Representatives elects its own officers. Its leader is called the speaker. *Each Congress lasts for two years. The speaker or chosen leader is the most powerful member of the House of Representatives.*

and shall have the sole power of impeachment.

Article I, Section 3, clause 1. The Senate of the United States shall be composed of two *senators* from each state, [chosen by the *legislature* thereof,] for six years; and each senator shall have one vote.

Article I, Section 3, clause 2. Immediately after they shall be assembled in consequence of the first election, they shall be divided as equally as may be into three classes. The seats of the senators of the first class shall be vacated at the expiration of the second year, of the second class at the expiration of the fourth year, and of the third class at the expiration of the sixth year, so that one-third may be chosen every second year; [and if vacancies happen by resignation, or otherwise, during the recess of the legislature of any state, the executive thereof may make temporary appointments until the next meeting of the legislature, which shall then fill such vacancies].

Article I, Section 3, clause 3. No person shall be a senator who shall not have attained to the age of thirty years, and been nine years a citizen of the United States, and who shall not, when elected, be an inhabitant of that state for which he shall be chosen.

Impeachment

Only the House of Representatives has the power to impeach. The power of impeachment is defined as the power to determine whether or not high officials in the executive and judicial department should be formally accused of doing something so bad while in office that they should no longer be allowed to serve in the public trust. *The House of Representatives does not conduct the actual trial. It merely files the formal accusation which means the accused will face a trial in the Senate. The senators will decide the guilt or innocence of the accused.*

Senators

The Senate Chamber has two senators from each state. Senators were chosen by the state legislatures under the original Constitution. Senators serve six-year terms and each has one vote. *The 17th Amendment determined that senators shall be elected by the people.*

Terms of Office Are Staggered

The terms of U.S. senators are arranged so that one-third of the senators are elected every two years. The first time Congress met, one-third were elected for two-year terms; one-third were elected for four-year terms and one-third elected for six-year terms. Thereafter all senators would serve six-year terms of office. The reason for this arrangement is so that the entire Senate is never elected in a single election.

Qualifications

To become a U.S. senator, one must:

1. be 30 years old
2. be a U.S. citizen for nine years
3. live in the state he or she represents

Article I, Section 3, clause 4. The vice president of the United States shall be president of the Senate, but shall have no vote, unless they be equally divided.

Article I, Section 3, clause 5. The Senate shall choose their other officers, and also a president *pro tempore*, in the absence of the vice president, or when he shall exercise the office of President of the United States.

Article I, Section 3, clause 6. The Senate shall have the sole power to try all impeachments. When sitting for that purpose, they shall be on oath or affirmation. When the President of the United States is tried, the Chief Justice shall preside: and no person shall be convicted without the concurrence of two-thirds of the members present.

Article I, Section 3, clause 7. Judgment in cases of impeachment shall not extend further than to removal from office, and disqualification to hold and enjoy any office of honor, trust or profit under the United States: but the party convicted shall nevertheless be liable and subject to indictment, trial, judgment and punishment, according to law.

Article I, Section 4, clause 1. The times, places and manner of holding elections for senators and representatives, shall be prescribed in each state by the legislature thereof; but the Congress may at any time by law make or alter such regulations, [except as to the places of choosing senators].

Senate Organization

The vice president of the United States presides over all meetings of the U.S. Senate and votes only when there is a tie.

Other Offices

The Senate chooses its other officers, including a *president pro tempore,* who will preside over the Senate when the vice president is unable to attend because of his or her duties as vice president.

Trying Impeachments

The Senate has the sole power to try those who have been impeached by members of the House of Representatives. The entire Senate serves as the jury and they take an oath that promises to try the accused fairly. If it is the President on trial, then the Chief Justice of the Supreme Court presides over the trial. Otherwise, the vice president presides. To convict the accused requires a two-thirds vote of all members present.

Extent of Punishment

In cases where the Senate finds the accused guilty, its power is limited to removing the official from office and preventing him or her from holding another office. But the convicted official can nevertheless be tried in a regular court of law, and if found guilty, could be punished according to the laws.

Election

All matters regarding times, places, and procedures of election are controlled by the state. But Congress can overrule any such state rule and establish rules of its own. Congress has determined that its members shall be elected on the Tuesday after the first Monday in November in all even-numbered years. This is called a *general election.* All elections are done by secret ballot. *The 17th Amendment changes the last part of the last sentence of clause 1—U.S. senators are now elected by the people just as representatives.*

Article I, Section 4, clause 2. The Congress shall assemble at least once in every year, [and such meeting shall be on the first Monday in December,] unless they shall by law appoint a different day.

Article I, Section 5, clause 1. Each house shall be the judge of the elections, returns and qualifications of its own members, and a majority of each shall constitute a quorum to do business; but a smaller number may adjourn from day to day, and may be authorized to compel the attendance of absent members, in such manner, and under such penalties as each house may provide.

Article I, Section 5, clause 2. Each house may determine the rules of its proceedings, punish its members for disorderly behavior, and, with the concurrence of two-thirds, expel a member.

Article I, Section 5, clause 3. Each house shall keep a journal of its proceedings, and from time to time publish the same, excepting such parts as may in their judgment require secrecy; and the yeas and nays of the members of either house on any question shall, at the desire of one-fifth of those present, be entered on the journal.

When Congress Meets

Congress meets once each year. The 20th Amendment changed the last part of clause 2 to January 3 as the date when Congress meets each year. With the exception of weekends, recesses and vacations, the meeting lasts most of the year.

Qualifications of Membership and Quorum Defined

In the case of a disputed election, each house can determine if its elected members are suitable and desirable. Even though a person has been duly elected by the people, the House or Senate has the right to refuse to seat that person if it feels he or she has engaged in activity that makes him or her unworthy of the honor. Neither house can meet unless it has a *quorum*. A quorum is defined as more than half the members present.

Membership Conduct

Each house shall make its own rules for conducting its affairs and punish its members who may break the rules. A member of either house may be expelled by a two-thirds vote of the members of that house.

Congressional Record

Both the House and the Senate keep records of what is said and done each day it meets. Certain proceedings can be kept secret if the membership desires, but a request by one-fifth of the members present can force all voting to be made public knowledge. In practice, every word that is said plus all legislation considered each day in Congress is published at the end of each day in the *Congressional Record*. Included are the results of all votes taken and how each member voted.

Article I, Section 5, clause 4. Neither house, during the session of Congress, shall, without the consent of the other, adjourn for more than three days, nor to any other place than that in which the two houses shall be sitting.

Article I, Section 6, clause 1. The senators and representatives shall receive a compensation for their services, to be ascertained by law, and paid out of the treasury of the United States. They shall in all cases, except treason, felony and breach of the peace, be privileged from arrest during their attendance at the session of their respective houses, and in going to and returning from the same; and for any speech or debate in either house, they shall not be questioned in any other place.

Article I, Section 6, clause 2. No senator or representative shall, during the time for which he was elected, be appointed to any civil office under the authority of the United States which shall have been created, or the emoluments whereof shall have been increased during such time; and no person holding any office under the United States, shall be a member of either house during his continuance in office.

Congress in Recess

During sessions of Congress, neither house can recess for more than three days without agreement from both houses. Both houses must also meet in the same city. *The purpose of this clause is to allow members of Congress to do their work without interference from those who might make meeting difficult through time and place restrictions and red tape. The city in which they meet is Washington, D.C.*

Membership Privileges

Members of Congress shall receive an annual salary paid out of the United States Treasury according to laws which they themselves establish. Members also enjoy freedom from arrest except for treason and serious crimes while meetings are in session. Also members can say what they want during all meetings, as nothing they may say can be held against them. *This paragraph was built into the Constitution so that members of Congress would not be intentionally prevented from meeting to vote on key issues.*

Membership Restrictions

Members of Congress cannot hold any other government offices or jobs while in office; nor can they resign while in office and take another job that was created while they were in office; nor can they take jobs for which the salary was increased while they were in office.

Legislative Department

Article I, Sections 1–3

1. What is the main content focus of Article 1? _____

_____

2. In a single sentence, describe the main function of the legislative department.

_____

_____

3. The two houses or chambers of the legislative branch are

_____ and _____.

4. The two houses together are called _____.

5. Complete the chart about the members of Congress.

Minimum Age Requirement:		
Citizenship Requirement:		
Residential Requirement:		
Term of Office:		
Number of Members:		

6. What is the title of the main officer in the U.S. House of Representatives?

_____

That office is currently filled by _____.

7. Who usually presides over the U.S. Senate? _____

Who presently holds that office? _____

8. What determines the number of representatives each state is entitled to have in the

   U.S. House of Representatives? _____

   Who is your Congressperson? _____

   How many representatives does your state have? _____

   What congressional district do you live in? _____

   Each state has two U.S. senators. Who are the senators for your state?

   _____ and _____

9. What happens in the event of a vacancy occurring in either chamber of
   Congress?

   _____

10. Explain why the framers of the Constitution designed a legislature composed of
    two houses.

    _____

    _____

    _____

    _____

11. What is the purpose of impeachment? _____

    _____

    Why was it made a part of the Constitution? _____

    _____

12. Why was the power given to Congress and what is the role played by each house in the impeachment process? _____

_____

House's Role	Senate's Role
_____	_____
_____	_____
_____	_____

13. What vote is necessary in the House to achieve an impeachment? _____

What vote is necessary in the Senate to get a conviction? _____

14. Which two presidents have been impeached?

_____ and _____

15. What was the nature of Andrew Johnson's alleged wrongdoing?

_____

What was the result of his trial in the Senate?

_____

16. Why would it be more appropriate for the Chief Justice of the Supreme Court to preside over an impeachment trial of a president instead of the vice president?

_____

_____

17. In 1974, President Richard Nixon was "almost impeached." What was the nature of his alleged wrongdoing and how did he escape impeachment?

_____

_____

_____

18. What was the nature of the charges brought against Bill Clinton that led to his

impeachment? _____

_____

What was the result of his trial in the Senate? _____

_____

19. Each house of Congress has some important leaders who have a great deal of power and importance in controlling party politics within their respective chambers. Find out the current name of each and indicate his party affiliation with *D* for Democrat and *R* for Republican.

House of Representatives	Senate
Speaker	Vice President
_____	_____
Majority Leader	president pro tempore
_____	_____
Majority Whip	Majority Whip
_____	_____
Minority Leader	Minority Leader
_____	_____
Minority Whip	Minority Whip
_____	_____

20. All meetings of Congress are identified by a number. What number is currently in session?

_____

Legislative Department

Article I, Sections 4–6

1. What day is established for congressional general elections?

    _____

2. On what date will the next general election be held?

    _____

3. On what date does Congress normally begin its annual meeting unless otherwise determined?

    _____

4. Why are voting booths and all the security associated with the secret ballot system necessary?

    _____

5   How is a quorum defined in Article 1, Section 5, as it applies to Congress?

    _____

    How many members constitute a quorum in each house?

    House of Representatives _____   Senate _____

6. Each house is responsible for the conduct of its own members. What vote is required by either house to expel a member of that house? _____ How many representatives would be required to expel a member of the House? _____ How many senators would be required to expel a senator from the Senate? _____

7. Do you think it is fair that the people of a congressional district might elect a candidate, then have the House of Representatives vote not to seat that person? Before you answer, think of the reason why the framers of the Constitution made this rule a part of the Constitution.

    _____

8. What fraction of either house of Congress is necessary to require voting in that house to be made public knowledge?

_____

9. Why is it appropriate for members of Congress to make it a matter of public knowledge the way they vote on laws and issues brought before Congress?

_____

10. The official minutes of Congress are published daily whenever Congress is in session. What is this official record called?

_____

11. What is the longest recess one house can take without the consent of the other?

_____

12. Why does Article 1, Section 5, clause 4 require that both houses must be in session at the same time?

_____

13. What is the current annual salary of members of Congress? Since members of Congress establish their own salaries, what would prevent them from voting themselves larger pay raises?

_____

14. Find out why the framers of the Constitution granted members of Congress freedom from arrest while Congress is in session except for serious crimes.

_____

15. Review Article 1, Section 6, clause 2. What would be wrong with having a member of Congress resign his or her office to take a newly created position in government if in fact he or she is well-qualified to fill that position?

_____

Government for the People

The members of both houses of Congress are there to serve us. After all, we are the reasons they have their jobs. It is thus their duty to serve our needs and see that our interests are protected. They do this by initiating laws and voting on laws that will be of help to us. They also should vote against laws that would not be good for us. A law that might benefit people in New York might be bad for people living in Wyoming. When an important law is being debated and is due for a vote, it is often helpful for these congresspeople to hear from the citizens they serve. Find out how to write to your representative and senators and list their mailing addresses below:

Representative	Senator	Senator
_____	_____	_____
_____	_____	_____
_____	_____	_____
_____	_____	_____

In the space that follows, write a letter to one of them explaining your position on a current issue of concern to you.

Article I, Section 7, clause 1. All bills for raising revenue shall originate in the House of Representatives; but the Senate may propose or concur with amendments as on other bills.

Article I, Section 7, clause 2. Every bill which shall have passed the House of Representatives and the Senate, shall, before it becomes a law, be presented to the President of the United States; if he approve he shall sign it, but if not he shall return it, with his objections to that house in which it shall have originated, who shall enter the objections at large on their journal, and proceed to reconsider it. If after such reconsideration two-thirds of that house shall agree to pass the bill, it shall be sent, together with the objections, to the other house, by which it shall likewise be reconsidered, and if approved by two-thirds of that house, it shall become a law. But in all such cases the votes of both houses shall be determined by yeas and nays, and the names of the persons voting for and against the bill shall be entered on the journal of each house respectively.

Revenue Bills

All bills involving the increasing of taxes to raise money must begin in the House of Representatives, but Senate approval is necessary for the bill to become a law. The Senate may also propose changes or amendments as it does on other bills. *The reason only the House has this power to initiate revenue bills goes back to the original Constitution in which only House members were elected by the people. Senators were chosen by the state legislatures and the writers of the Constitution did not want laws involving money started by people who had not been elected by the people.*

Presidential Veto

Once a bill has successfully been approved by both the House and the Senate, it is sent on to the President for his* approval. If he approves, he signs it and the bill will become a law. If he does not approve, he returns it unsigned to the house where it originated along with his objection. If that house wishes to keep the bill just as it was, then two-thirds of the members present must vote in its favor. If this happens, the bill is then sent on to the other house. If two-thirds of the members present favor the bill, then the bill will become a law despite the President's veto.

*For simplicity, the pronoun *he* is used when referring to the President of the United States and the vice president. Use of the male pronoun is not intended to imply that the office is limited to the male gender.

If any bill shall not be returned by the President within ten days (Sundays excepted) after it shall have been presented to him, the same shall be a law, in like manner as if he had signed it, unless the Congress by their adjournment prevent its return, in which case it shall not be a law.

Article 1, Section 7, clause 3. Every order, resolution, or vote to which the concurrence of the Senate and House of Representatives may be necessary (except on a question of adjournment) shall be presented to the President of the United States; and before the same shall take effect, shall be approved by him, or being disapproved by him, shall be repassed by two-thirds of the Senate and House of Representatives, according to the rules and limitations prescribed in the case of a bill.

Failure of President to Act on Bill

The President has ten days (not counting Sundays) to act on legislation once he has been sent a bill approved by Congress. If he fails to sign or veto the bill within that time, then the bill becomes a law without his signature. If Congress adjourns during this time, then the President doesn't have to act on the bill because it won't become a law if he fails to sign it. Such failure to act by the President is called a pocket veto. *Congress passes many bills daily that do not affect the general public. For lack of time, the President often does nothing about these bills, because he knows that the unsigned bills will become laws anyway.*

Orders and Resolutions of Congress

Any other orders, resolutions, or votes by Congress (except the matter of adjournment) require the President's approval. If the President vetoes the action by Congress, it takes a two-thirds vote of both houses of Congress to override his veto.

How a Bill Becomes a Law

A bill can start in either house of Congress. Only bills dealing with revenue must start in the House of Representatives. If a proposed law (bill) fails to achieve the required approval anywhere along the way, the bill dies. To become a law, a bill must follow the route outlined below.

An idea for a new law may begin in the mind of anyone—from an individual citizen, even the president. A bill can only be presented before Congress by a member of Congress. **1**	**The committee then votes. If the committee approves, the bill goes before the full House or Senate (depending on where the bill was initiated).** **5**
The congressperson presents the idea to his or her staff, and the rough idea is refined into a proposed bill. **2**	**That house of Congress votes. If the bill passes by a simple majority, the bill is sent on to the other house.** **6**
The congressperson then presents the bill before other members of the house of Congress to which he or she belongs. **3**	**The proper committee receives the bill and studies the bill much the same as the committee in the other house did.** **7**
The bill is then sent to its appropriate committee where it is studied. Hearings are held and evidence gathered to decide if the bill has merit. The committee can add or delete as it sees fit. **4**	**Once all the evidence is in and any changes are made, the committee votes. If it approves, the bill is brought before the full house of Congress.** **8**

How a Bill Becomes a Law

The second house then votes on the bill. If it passes by a simple majority, it is sent with its changes back to the house where it started.

9

If the President signs the bill, it becomes the law of the land.

13

That first house then considers any changes that were made. If it approves of all the changes, the bill is sent on to the President.

10

If the President does not approve, he vetoes the bill and it is returned to the house where it originated.

14

If this house where the bill originated feels some compromise is in order, a committee from both houses rewrites certain parts of the bill.

11

If the bill gets a two-thirds majority approval in the house where it started, the bill is sent on to the other house.

15

The bill including all the changes is then voted upon once again by both houses. If it achieves a simple majority in both houses, it is sent on to the President.

12

If the other house approves by a two-thirds majority, the bill becomes a law overriding the President's veto.

16

Teacher Note: Pages 43 and 44 show how a bill becomes a law. Reproduce both pages and have students cut out the pieces and arrange them in correct order. Cover the numbers before reproducing to make the activity more challenging.

Charting HB-1117

After studying the various steps necessary for a bill to become a law, briefly summarize these steps in your own words so that you will remember them. Build a chart of your own or simply list the steps.

Summary of how a bill becomes a law

Build a flow chart showing the path followed by HB-1117, which eventually becomes a law despite the President's veto.

Flow chart for HB-1117

Expressing Disapproval

1. Once a proposed bill has been presented formally before Congress, it becomes news and the people begin hearing and reading about it in the media. At this point, how can the public express its dissatisfaction with or its support for a proposed bill?

   _____

   _____

2. What is the difference between a pocket veto and a normal veto registered by the President?

   _____

   _____

   Are there any differences in the effects of the two? _____

3. If the President vetoes a bill, what effect might that have on the members of his political party in Congress when they review the bill?

   _____

   _____

4. Why does the President sometimes allow the ten days he has to sign a bill into law to expire without doing anything?

   _____

   _____

5. Why do you think the framers of the Constitution gave the President the power to veto a law passed by Congress? What do you think might happen if the President did not have this power?

   _____

   _____

Express Powers of Congress

Article I, Section 8, clause 1. The Congress shall have power: To lay and collect taxes, duties, imposts and excises, to pay the debts and provide for the common defense and general welfare of the United States; but all duties, imposts and excises shall be uniform throughout the United States;

Congress has the power to collect taxes to pay debts, provide for an adequate defense and provide services for the good of all the people. All duties on imports and excise taxes must be the same throughout the country.

Article I, Section 8, clause 2. To borrow money on the credit of the United States;

Congress has the power to borrow money.

Article I, Section 8, clause 3. To regulate commerce with foreign nations, and among the several states, and with the Indian tribes;

Congress has the power to regulate trade, both foreign and domestic. *Domestic trade is defined as trade among states within the United States.*

Article I, Section 8, clause 4. To establish a uniform rule of naturalization, and uniform laws on the subject of bankruptcies throughout the United States;

Congress establishes rules on foreign-born persons becoming citizens of the United States. Congress also makes the rules regarding bankruptcies. *Naturalization is defined as making a foreign-born person a citizen of the United States. Bankruptcy occurs when a person builds his debts to a point far beyond his ability to pay them. When this happens, the courts take his property and split it up among his creditors.*

Article I, Section 8, clause 5. To coin money, regulate the value thereof, and of foreign coin, and fix the standard of weights and measures;

Congress has the power to coin money, establish its worth and determine the value of foreign money in U.S. dollars. Congress also sets the standards for weights and measures within the United States.

Article I, Section 8, clause 6. To provide for the punishment of counterfeiting the securities and current coin of the United States;

Congress has the power to punish those who counterfeit U.S. money and bonds. *Counterfeiting is defined as making fake money or U. S. bonds.*

Article I, Section 8, clause 7. To establish post offices and post roads;

Congress establishes all U.S. post offices and highways.

Article I, Section 8, clause 8. To promote the progress of science and useful arts, by securing for limited times to authors and inventors the exclusive rights to their respective writings and discoveries;

Congress promotes the progress of science and the arts by passing patent and copyright laws that will protect the inventors and authors from being copied by others. *Patents are issued to inventors to protect their inventions; copyrights are issued to authors and composers who write books and music.*

Article I, Section 8, clause 9. To constitute tribunals inferior to the Supreme Court;

Congress has the power to establish courts beneath the Supreme Court as needed.

Article I, Section 8, clause 10. To define and punish piracies and felonies committed on the high seas, and offenses against the law of nations;

Congress has the power to make laws and punish those who break those laws on all U.S. waters. Also Congress can punish those who break international laws on our waters.

Article I, Section 8, clause 11. To declare war, grant letters of marque and reprisal, and make rules concerning captures on land and water;

Congress has the power to declare war and make rules concerning the seizure of enemy property. *Letters of marque were permission granted to private persons to allow them to capture enemy ships in exchange for being allowed to keep the captured cargo. It was later agreed by international law for nations to stop this practice of encouraging legalized piracy.*

Article I, Section 8, clause 12. To raise and support armies, but no appropriation of money to that use shall be for a longer term than two years;

Congress has the power to raise and support an army, but no money may be appropriated for its support for more than two years at a time.

Article I, Section 8, clause 13. To provide and maintain a navy;

Congress has the power to raise and support a navy.

Article I, Section 8, clause 14. To make rules for the government and regulation of the land and naval forces;

Congress has the power to make rules that regulate and control its army and navy.

Article I, Section 8, clause 15. To provide for calling forth the militia to execute the laws of the Union, suppress insurrections and repel invasions;

Congress has the power to call forth state militia to help enforce the law, to quiet any riots and violence and to drive out invaders. *In practice these state militias, called the National Guard, are most often used to help in times of natural disasters— floods, tornadoes, hurricanes, etc.*

Article I, Section 8, clause 16. To provide for organizing, arming, and disciplining the militia, and for governing such part of them as may be employed in the service of the United States, reserving to the states respectively, the appointment of the officers, and the authority of training the militia according to the discipline prescribed by Congress;

Congress has the power to provide for the organizing, training, and disciplining of the soldiers in that state militia. But the states have the power to choose the officers of their National Guards and to train them according to the rules established by Congress.

Article I, Section 8, clause 17. To exercise exclusive legislation in all cases whatsoever, over such district (not exceeding ten miles square) as may, by cession of particular states, and the acceptance of Congress, become the seat of the government of the United States, and to exercise like authority over all places purchased by the consent of the legislature of the state in which the same shall be for the erection of forts, magazines, arsenals, dockyards, and other needful buildings;

Congress has the power to make all the laws for the national capital (Washington, D.C.). That district to be governed is not to exceed 10 miles square. Congress shall exercise power over all places bought from the states for use as forts, arsenals, navy yards, and public buildings. *The framers of the Constitution did not want the national capital to be in any state. As a result, Virginia and Maryland gave up land where the two came together to form the present-day center of our national government— Washington, D.C.*

 076822456X • Our Living Constitution

Express Powers of Congress

Write which clause of Article 1, Section 8 gives Congress the power to act in each of the following situations:

1. _____ establish a post office in Ferris, Illinois

2. _____ issue a patent to Kent Hamilton to protect the design of his new solar collector

3. _____ set the minimum prison sentence for those found guilty of counterfeiting U.S. currency

4. _____ authorize a new issue of government bonds

5. _____ determine the rules governing Carlo Ferraro's request for U.S. citizenship

6. _____ raise the tax on imported foreign cars to help stimulate the American automobile industry

7. _____ fix the penalties for those found guilty of violating laws on U.S. seas

8. _____ call out the National Guard units to restore law and order following a violent protest

9. _____ declare war on a foreign nation that has attacked the United States

10. _____ authorize spending money to keep active a fleet of warships ready to defend the United States

11. _____ determine the city sales tax on purchases made in the city of Washington, D.C.

12. _____ authorize positions for ten more federal district judges

13. _____ establish 18 as the minimum age for the army and navy

14. _____ establish a set of rules for training members of the National Guard

15. _____ authorize the defense budget for the next year

16. _____ arrange for Russia to buy 20 million metric tons of wheat from American farmers

17. _____ authorize the issuing of a $2.00 coin

Implied Power

These first seventeen clauses of Article 1, Section 8 point specifically to powers the framers of the Constitution felt Congress should have. They are referred to as the *express* powers of Congress. But the men who wrote the Constitution were smart enough to realize that new areas of concern would emerge on which Congress must act. Thus the framers placed this last paragraph in Section 8, known as the elastic clause. It gives Congress implied power to act in areas not specifically cited in the first 17 clauses and has had the effect of providing a great deal of additional strength for Congress.

Article I, Section 8, clause 18. And to make all laws which shall be necessary and proper for carrying into execution the foregoing powers, and all other powers vested by this Constitution in the government of the United States, or in any department or officer thereof.

Congress shall have the power to make all laws necessary to enforce the powers granted it in the first 17 clauses. It shall also make laws needed to carry out powers granted to the government by this Constitution. *Congress must still work within the powers of the Constitution. It cannot simply make any laws it desires. There are also checks against this power through the veto of the President and the ability of the Supreme Court to rule laws unconstitutional which fall outside the framework of the Constitution.*

Cite several examples in today's world where Congress has exercised implied power. Look in newspapers and magazines for additional ideas. Use a separate sheet of paper if necessary.

_____

_____

_____

List some powers you feel Congress should have that are not listed in Article 1, Section 8.

_____

_____

_____

Name_____

Express vs. Implied Power

In teams of two to four students, prepare an answer for each of the questions below.

1. Explain the difference between the *express* and *implied* powers contained in Section 8, and provide examples to support the strength that clause 18 gives to Congress.

_____

_____

2. Article 1, Section 8, clause 2 gives Congress the power to borrow money. How does it go about borrowing this money?

_____

_____

3. Research the requirements that must be satisfied for a foreign-born person to become a naturalized U.S. citizen.

_____

_____

4. What is the difference between patents and copyrights?

_____

_____

What purpose do they serve?

_____

_____

Think about 10 real-life examples of how Congress has used the powers given to it in Article 1, Section 8. Write each example on its own 3" x 5" index card. On the back of the card, write whether your example is one of Congress' express powers or implied powers. Trade cards with another group. Look at their cards, and without looking at the backs, tell which type of power is being exercised in each example.

Article I, Section 9, clause 1. The migration or importation of such persons as any of the states now existing shall think proper to admit, shall not be prohibited by the Congress prior to the year one thousand eight hundred and eight, but a tax or duty may be imposed on such importation, not exceeding ten dollars for each person.

Article I, Section 9, clause 2. The privilege of the writ of *habeas corpus* shall not be suspended, unless when in cases of rebellion or invasion the public safety may require it.

Article I, Section 9, clause 3. No bill of attainder or *ex post facto* law shall be passed.

Article I, Section 9, clause 4. No capitation, [or other direct,] tax shall be laid, unless in proportion to the census or enumeration herein before directed to be taken.

Prohibitions on Congress

Prior to 1808, Congress could make no law forbidding slave trade. It could, however, impose a tax of $10 per slave on those brought into this country. *This clause was a part of the original compromise that led to agreement on the Constitution. Those who favored slave trading avoided an absolute prohibition of slavery. Those who opposed slave trading accepted the twenty-year delay because the issue could be reviewed then.*

Writs of habeas corpus can only be suspended when the nation is in rebellion or being invaded by a foreign nation. *A writ of habeas corpus is a court order directing that a person accused of committing a crime be brought before the court to determine if he is being legally detained.*

Congress cannot pass bills of attainder (laws made to punish particular individuals) nor ex post facto laws (making it illegal to have done something that was not against the law when it was done). *These kinds of things had been done by King George to jail those in the colonies who caused him trouble, and the framers of the Constitution wanted to prevent it from ever happening again.*

All taxes levied by Congress must be the same for all people living in the United States. Other direct taxes shall be based on population. *The 16th Amendment made it legal to tax individuals according to their wealth (income tax).*

Article I, Section 9, clause 5. No tax or duty shall be laid on articles exported from any state.

Congress shall not tax goods exported from any state.

Article I, Section 9, clause 6. No preference shall be given by any regulation of commerce or revenue to the ports of one state over those of another: nor shall vessels bound to, or from, one state, be obliged to enter, clear, or pay duties in another.

Congress cannot pass laws that show preference for one state over another. Ships may travel on the waters of other states without paying duties. *This clause was put in the Constitution to avoid the quarrels that developed under the Articles of Confederation which allowed each state to make its own trade laws. Under that arrangement, states began to charge unfair rates that often made the shipping charges cost more than the goods were worth.*

Article I, Section 9, clause 7. No money shall be drawn from the treasury, but in consequence of appropriations made by law; and a regular statement and account of the receipts and expenditures of all public money shall be published from time to time.

No money can be drawn from the U.S. Treasury unless authorized by Congress and a regular accounting of all dollars spent must be made available to the public.

Article I, Section 9, clause 8. No title of nobility shall be granted by the United States: And no person holding any office of profit or trust under them, shall, without the consent of the Congress, accept of any present, emolument, office, or title, of any kind whatsoever, from any king, prince, or foreign state.

No titles of nobility (for example, king, queen, princess, duke) shall be granted by the U.S. government; nor can anyone in the service of our government be allowed to accept a title from a foreign power.

Prohibitions on the States

Article I, Section 10, clause 1. No state shall enter into any treaty, alliance, or confederation;

No state can make a treaty with a foreign country;

grant letters of marque and reprisal;

grant private citizens the right to capture ships from other countries;

coin money; emit bills of credit;

coin its own money;

make anything but gold and silver coin a tender in payment of debts;

use anything other than gold or silver as a standard of money;

pass any bill of attainder;

pass a bill of attainder (laws declaring a specific person guilty of breaking the law);

ex post facto law,

pass an ex post facto law (law that would punish someone for doing something that was not illegal when it was done);

or law impairing the obligation of contracts,

pass laws that excuse people from their legal obligations under contract law;

or grant any title of nobility.

grant titles of nobility.

Article I, Section 10, clause 2. No state shall, without the consent of the Congress, lay any imposts or duties on imports or exports, except what may be absolutely necessary for executing its inspection laws: and the net produce of all duties and imposts, laid by any state on imports or exports, shall be for the use of the treasury of the United States; and all such laws shall be subject to the revision and control of the Congress.

No state may place a tax on goods imported or exported, without the approval of Congress. However, an inspection fee may be charged. Any import or export taxes approved by Congress must go into the United States Treasury.

Article I, Section 10, clause 3. No state shall, without the consent of Congress, lay any duty of tonnage, keep troops, or ships of war in time of peace, enter into any agreement or compact with another state, or with a foreign power, or engage in war, unless actually invaded, or in such imminent danger as will not admit of delay.

No state may tax ships or keep troops or ships during peacetime, make treaties with other states or foreign countries, or go to war unless attacked and in such danger that delay would be harmful to the state.

What Congress Cannot Do

1. What is the difference between an ex post facto law and a bill of attainder?

_____

_____

Both sound so unfair that it makes one wonder why the framers of the Constitution would even bother mentioning them. Why did they include this paragraph?

_____

_____

2. What is a writ of habeas corpus?

_____

3. What was the purpose of Article 1, Section 9, clause 1?

_____

_____

4. Define *letters of marque* and tell why you think Congress was forbidden from granting them under the Constitution.

_____

_____

5. Why do you think titles of nobility were outlawed by the Constitution?

_____

_____

6. How did the 16th Amendment to the Constitution modify Article 1, Section 9, clause 4?

_____

_____

Article II – Executive Department

Article 2 presents the powers and duties of the Chief Executive. The President is responsible for enforcing the laws made by Congress. Article 2 of the Constitution outlines the powers and rules of the presidency. You will see why some of the rules the framers of the Constitution set did not work and were later changed by amending the Constitution.

Article II, Section 1, clause 1. The executive power shall be vested in a President of the United States of America. He shall hold his office during the term of four years, and, together with the Vice President, chosen for the same term, be elected as follows:

Article II, Section 1, clause 2. Each state shall appoint, in such manner as the legislature thereof may direct, a number of electors, equal to the whole number of senators and representatives to which the state may be entitled in the Congress: but no senator or representative, or person holding an office of trust or profit under the United States, shall be appointed an elector.

President Defined

The executive power (the power to execute the laws) shall be held by the President of the United States. The President shall serve a four-year term of office. There will also be a vice president elected at the same time for the same term of office.

Electors Elect the President

The President is elected by *electors.* The electors in each state are chosen in the manner prescribed by the state legislatures. Each state is entitled to a number of electors equal to its number of senators and representatives in Congress. But representatives and senators are not allowed to be electors themselves. It is these electors who actually choose the President. *Many people could not read and write at the time the Constitution was written. They were also poorly informed on matters of the day because there was no media to speak of. Thus the framers of the Constitution felt that the election of the President should be placed in the hands of a few who knew the candidates and what each represented. It didn't take long, however, for the various state legislatures to allow the people to choose their electors and eventually it became as it is today. The electors collectively are called the Electoral College, and they still actually elect the President. But the people in each state vote on who will become their electors, depending on who they want to be their President. Thus, in reality, it is the people who are electing the President.*

Article II, Section 1, clause 3. The electors shall meet in their respective states, and vote by ballot for two persons, of whom one at least shall not be an inhabitant of the same state with themselves. And they shall make a list of all the persons voted for, and of the number of votes for each; which list they shall sign and certify, and transmit sealed to the seat of the government of the United States, directed to the president of the Senate. The president of the Senate shall, in the presence of the Senate and House of Representatives, open all the certificates, and the votes shall then be counted. The person having the greatest number of votes shall be the President, if such number be a majority of the whole number of electors appointed; and if there be more than one who have such majority, and have an equal number of votes, then the House of Representatives shall immediately choose by ballot one of them for President; and if no person have a majority, then from the five highest on the list the said House shall in like manner choose the President. But in choosing the President, the votes shall be taken by states, the representation from each state having one vote; a quorum for this purpose shall consist of a member or members from two-thirds of the states, and a majority of all the states shall be necessary to a choice. In every case, after the choice of the President, the person having the greatest number of votes of the electors shall be the vice president. But if there should remain two or more who have equal votes, the Senate shall choose from them by ballot the vice president.

Method of Election

This paragraph tells how the President was originally elected. Keep in mind that this method was changed by the 12th Amendment (see page 109). The electors met in their states and voted for two people, one of whom had to live in another state. A list was then compiled of all those receiving votes and the number of votes each received. The lists were opened before a joint session of Congress. The person having the greatest number of votes became President. If more than one person achieved a majority with the same number of votes, the House of Representatives would choose between those two candidates. If no one person achieved a majority, then the House of Representatives chose the President from the five who had the most votes. In such elections, each state shall have one vote and two-thirds of the states must be present. After the choice for the President was made, the electors chose the vice president. He was the person who came in second in the election for the presidency. If there was a tie for vice president, the Senate would elect the vice president.

Article II, Section 1, clause 4. The Congress may determine the time of choosing the electors, and the day on which they shall give their votes; which day shall be the same throughout the United States.

Article II, Section 1, clause 5. No person except a natural-born citizen, or a citizen of the United States at the time of the adoption of this Constitution, shall be eligible to the office of President; neither shall any person be eligible to that office who shall not have attained to the age of thirty-five years, and been fourteen years a resident within the United States.

Article II, Section 1, clause 6. In case of the removal of the President from office, or of his death, resignation, or inability to discharge the powers and duties of the said office, the same shall devolve on the Vice President, and the Congress may by law provide for the case of removal, death, resignation or inability, both of the President and Vice President, declaring what officer shall then act as President, and such officer shall act accordingly, until the disability be removed, or a President shall be elected.

Article II, Section 1, clause 7. The President shall, at stated times, receive for his services, a compensation, which shall neither be increased nor diminished during the period for which he shall have been elected, and he shall not receive within that period any other emolument from the United States, or any of them.

When Electors Are Chosen

Congress shall determine the date when electors will be chosen. *That date has come to be the Tuesday after the first Monday in November in all years evenly divisible by four. The Electoral College then cast their votes on the Monday after the second Wednesday in December following the November elections.*

Qualifications for President

To become President of the United States, one must:

1. be a natural-born U.S. citizen
2. be at least 35 years of age
3. have lived in the United States for 14 years

Vacancy in the Presidency

In the event of a vacancy occurring in the presidency, the vice president would assume the duties of the President. Congress would then decide by law who would be next in line should the vice president also become unable to serve as President. *This line of succession to the presidency and the procedures involving the vice president assuming the duties of the President have been changed and more clearly defined by the 25th Amendment.*

Rules Affecting the President's Salary

The President shall receive a salary which cannot be raised nor lowered during his term of office. The President may not receive any other salary from the United States or from any state while he is in office.

Article II, Section 1, clause 8. Before he enter on the execution of his office, he shall take the following oath or affirmation: "I do solemnly swear (or affirm) that I will faithfully execute the office of President of the United States, and will to the best of my ability, preserve, protect and defend the Constitution of the United States."

The Oath of Office

Before becoming President, the person elected to the position must take the following oath of office: "I do solemnly swear (or affirm) that I will faithfully execute the office of President of the United States and will to the best of my ability preserve, protect and defend the Constitution of the United States." *This condition of office (accepting this oath) is usually administered by the Chief Justice of the Supreme Court at the President's inauguration, which usually occurs on January 20.*

Executive Department

Article II, Section 1

Below are the answers to a crossword puzzle containing some important words in Article 2, Section 1. Make up the clues that go with the answers.

Clues:

1. _____ 6. _____

2. _____ 7. _____

3. _____ 8. _____

4. _____ 9. _____

5. _____ 10. _____

1. Why did the framers of the Constitution create the electoral system?

_____

_____

_____

_____

2. Under the original Constitution, what was wrong with the method used for choosing the President and vice president?

_____

_____

_____

How did the 12th Amendment correct this problem?

_____

_____

3. What is the purpose of Article 2, Section 1, clause 7? What might happen if the President's salary could be adjusted by Congress while he is in office?

_____

_____

_____

_____

4. In 1984, Geraldine Ferraro ran as the vice-presidential candidate with Walter Mondale on the Democratic party ticket. They did not win but many considered Ms. Ferraro's running a giant stride toward having a woman for our President. What are your own views about a woman becoming Chief Executive?

_____

_____

_____

_____

_____

_____

A Man of Many Hats

It has often been said that the President of the United States has the "toughest job in the world." He must make careful decisions and take action on issues that will affect millions of people. The job of president involves successfully juggling many different roles. Some of these roles are summarized below.

Head of State: He is the living symbol of this nation, and he must provide an inspiring example for the American people.

Chief Executive: He is responsible for enforcing the laws of the United States as well as being in charge of the thousands of government workers within the Executive Department.

Chief Foreign Policy Maker: With the help of his advisors, he establishes foreign policy and decides how America will react to certain foreign issues.

Commander in Chief: He is in charge of the Army, the Navy, the Air Force and the Marines.

Chief Legislator: Although Congress makes the laws, the president has a great deal of influence in deciding which legislation will be passed.

Chief of Party: He is also the leader of his political party. He must constantly be campaigning for others in his party who are running for office.

Watchdog of the Economy: His role here is to do his best to fight inflation and to create a prosperous U.S. economy. He also prepares the nation's budget.

Presidential Duties

Determine which role the President is performing in each of the following situations. The President may perform more than one role at a time. Write the letter on the line before each statement.

A. Chief Executive   E. Chief Foreign Policy Maker

B. Commander in Chief   F. Head of State

C. Chief of Party   G. Chief Legislator

D. Watchdog of the Economy

1. _____ Making a patriotic speech on Memorial Day

2. _____ Signing a bill sent to him by Congress

3. _____ Sending in the National Guard to help flood victims in Florida

4. _____ Traveling to Iowa to make a speech at a benefit dinner for a party nominee to Congress

5. _____ Meeting with labor leaders to discuss a strike by auto workers

6. _____ Hosting a summit meeting between hostile nations

7. _____ Holding a meeting in the White House for the leaders of the House Ways and Means Committee

8. _____ Awarding commissions to those who have recently graduated from West Point

9. _____ Choosing a member of his party to serve in the capacity of Secretary of Education

10. _____ Delivering his annual State of the Union message before the Congress

11. _____ Nominating someone to fill a vacancy created in a federal judgeship

12. _____ Officially receiving the Prime Minister of England

13. _____ Releasing 9,000 government workers he feels are no longer necessary

14 _____ Meeting with Arab oil leaders to help establish a more stable price for oil

15. _____ Commuting to life imprisonment the death sentence of a terrorist who set off a bomb in a Denver airport terminal

Electing the President

The men who wrote the Constitution planned for the two candidates with the most votes to become President and vice president. This theory was fine until political parties began to emerge. When this happened, the 12th Amendment became necessary. It was ratified in 1804, and since then each political party runs one candidate for president and one for vice president. The framers of the Constitution did not feel that the people were qualified to vote for their President. Rather, the President was elected by the Electoral College, which was made up of the electors from each state.

The number of electors for each state was equal to the number of representatives it had in the House of Representatives plus two (the number of U.S. senators in each state).

As the country grew and more states were added, more electors were included in the Electoral College. That number of electors was eventually frozen at 535. In 1961, the 23rd Amendment granted the citizens of Washington, D.C., the privilege of voting for President, too. That added three more electors (the minimum number a state can have) to the Electoral College, making the total 538. At the beginning of each decade, a census is taken. Any major population shifts can result in some states gaining some electors and other states losing some electors.

1. Use an almanac, encyclopedia, or the Internet to find the number of electors in each state for the last presidential election. Place those numbers within the boundaries of the states on the map on page 66.

2. How many electors did your state have in the last election? _____

3. Which candidate did your state vote for in the last election? _____

4. How many electors must a candidate have to win the presidency? _____

5. If you were running for president, in which states would you spend most of your time and money campaigning? Why? _____

_____

_____

Electoral Map of the United States

All the President's Men and Women

Without help from thousands of other people, the President would never get his job done. He forms a group called a *cabinet* consisting of his closest advisors. Each advisor, called a Secretary, is in charge of one particular area of concern to the people of the United States. The hundreds of people in that department are responsible for gathering information and resolving issues in that area. The Secretary is then responsible for keeping the President informed of the work within his or her department.

Do some research to find the duties of these various cabinet posts and then to match them with the statements given on the next page. Then name the Secretary who currently heads each department.

_____ 1. Department of Health and Human Services _____

_____ 2. Department of the Treasury _____

_____ 3. Department of Justice—Attorney General _____

_____ 4. Department of Defense _____

_____ 5. Department of the Interior _____

_____ 6. Department of Energy _____

_____ 7. Department of State _____

_____ 8. Department of Agriculture _____

_____ 9. Department of Transportation _____

_____10. Department of Housing and Urban Development _____

_____11. Department of Labor _____

_____12. Department of Commerce _____

_____13. Department of Education _____

_____14. Department of Veterans Affairs _____

a. This man or woman is mainly responsible for promoting all phases of commerce, industry, and business.

b. This person is responsible for managing our nation's finances, for the coining and printing of money, as well as enforcing all money laws. He or she is also responsible for the Secret Service and the Coast Guard.

c. This cabinet member is responsible for enforcing the laws of the United States in the federal courts. He or she is concerned with those legal matters in which the United States as a nation is involved. He or she is the chief legal officer and conducts investigations into monopolies, antitrust laws, organized crime, and the violation of conservation laws.

d. The head of this department is charged with keeping a reasonable and proper balance of all the nation's resources, and preserving scenic and historical landmarks. He or she is in charge of all National Parks and Forests, the Bureau of Indian Affairs, and the nation's water supply.

e. This person handles all of our foreign affairs, including the participation of the United States in the United Nations. He or she is also responsible for issuing passports and maintaining our foreign embassies. This cabinet member is perhaps the single most important of the cabinet members.

f. The Public Health Service, the Social Security Administration, the Food and Drug Administration, and the Office of Vocational Rehabilitation are a part of this department.

g. This department leader deals primarily with the complex transportation issues that face our ever-growing nation.

h. The responsibilities of this department center around the needs of those living in large metropolitan areas.

i. This secretary's authority extends to all of the armed forces. In addition, he or she advises the President on the budget for research and development of defense systems.

j. This department is responsible for all levels of education from the kindergarten level through the postgraduate level.

k. The head of this department continually analyzes our present and future energy reserves. He or she is in charge of implementing a national energy conservation program.

l. This person manages the nation's agricultural programs. He or she is concerned with getting a fair price for the American farmer's crops and in stimulating sales of U.S. agricultural products to foreign countries.

m. The leader of this department is in charge of the nation's labor supply. He or she tries to maintain a balance between the available supplies of human labor and the demand for it.

n. The person in charge of this department is responsible for maintaining all rights and benefits due to Americans who have served their country in the armed forces.

Military and Civil Powers of the President

Article II, Section 2, clause 1. The President shall be commander in chief of the Army and Navy of the United States, and of the militia of the several states, when called into the actual service of the United States; he may require the opinion, in writing, of the principal officer in each of the executive departments, upon any subject relating to the duties of their respective offices, and he shall have power to grant reprieves and pardons for offenses against the United States, except in cases of impeachment.

The President shall be commander in chief of the armed forces. He also commands the National Guard when they are called into the service of the United States. He is also in command of all the executive departments and may require them to report to him in writing of the progress and actions going on within their departments. He also has the power to grant reprieves and pardons for those convicted of federal crimes with the exception of cases involving impeachments. *In this paragraph, two of the President's main roles are assigned. The writers of the Constitution wanted him in charge of the armed forces because they preferred a civilian rather than a military person controling the nation's army and navy. He is also the chief executive; and the heads of departments who report to him have come to be known as his cabinet. They are his chief advisors.*

Article II, Section 2, clause 2. He shall have power, by and with the advice and consent of the Senate, to make treaties, provided two-thirds of the senators present concur;

and he shall nominate, and by and with the advice and consent of the Senate, shall appoint ambassadors, other public ministers and consuls, judges of the Supreme Court, and all other officers of the United States, whose appointments are not herein otherwise provided for, and which shall be established by law:

but the Congress may by law vest the appointment of such inferior officers, as they think proper, in the President alone, in the courts of law, or in the heads of departments.

Article II, Section 2, clause 3. The President shall have power to fill up all vacancies that may happen during the recess of the Senate, by granting commissions which shall expire at the end of their next session.

Treaties and Appointments

The President shall have the power to make agreements (treaties) with foreign nations. These agreements must be approved by two-thirds of the senators present when the agreement is voted on in the Senate. He also has the power to nominate ambassadors to foreign nations, Supreme Court justices, and other high-ranking government officials. His appointments must be approved by a simple majority of the senators present. Congress may, by law, allow the President the power to appoint lesser-ranking officials without approval from the Senate, or Congress may allow the courts or the heads of departments to appoint these officials. *This paragraph says a lot though it's not very long. It outlines the President's role of chief foreign policy maker and gives him the power to make treaties. It also empowers him to choose his own staff of advisors (cabinet), the important federal judges, foreign ambassadors, and other high-ranking officials. The framers of the Constitution built flexibility into the establishment of the bureaucracy by providing methods for choosing many government workers. Thousands of these employees are chosen through the Civil Service Commission.*

Temporary Appointments

The President has the power to fill vacancies as they occur while the Senate is in recess. These temporary appointments expire at the end of the next session of Congress.

Article II, Section 3. He shall from time to time give to the Congress information of the state of the Union, and recommend to their consideration such measures as he shall judge necessary and expedient;

he may, on extraordinary occasions, convene both houses, or either of them, and in case of disagreement between them, with respect to the time of adjournment, he may adjourn them to such time as he shall think proper;

he shall receive ambassadors and other public ministers;

he shall take care that the laws be faithfully executed, and shall commission all the officers of the United States.

Article II, Section 4. The President, Vice President and all civil officers of the United States, shall be removed from office on impeachment for, and conviction of, treason, bribery, or other high crimes and misdemeanors.

Duties of the President

The President shall address Congress from time to time on his assessment of the state of the nation. His annual message to them and to the people of the United States at the beginning of each session of Congress is called the State of the Union message. He shall recommend to Congress the legislation he wants them to consider making law. He can also call Congress into special session when he feels it necessary to the best interests of the nation. He may decide when Congress shall adjourn if they are in disagreement. He shall serve as the official host to receive foreign ambassadors and ministers. Finally, he has the responsibility for seeing that all laws are enforced, and he commissions all officers of the United States. *This clause is another that is loaded with importance to the power of the presidency. His recommendations to Congress place him in the role of our chief legislator. As the head of state, he receives the official heads of foreign nations. He serves as our chief executive when he sees that all laws of this country are faithfully executed and enforced.*

Removal from Office

The President, vice president, and other civil officers of the United States government can be removed from office if they are first impeached by the House of Representatives, then found guilty and convicted by the Senate. The grounds for such charges and convictions are only treason, bribery, or other high crimes and misdemeanors. *Treason is defined as providing aid to the enemy. High crimes are those considered serious crimes, and misdemeanors are less important crimes.*

Executive Department

Article II, Sections 2-4

Below are some important facts to remember from Article 2. Construct a question that can be answered with each phrase provided.

1. to enforce the laws _____
   _____
   _____

2. the President of the United States
   _____
   _____

3. Chief Executive _____
   _____
   _____

4. Commander in Chief _____
   _____
   _____

5. four years _____
   _____
   _____

6. vice president _____
   _____
   _____

7. number of representatives plus number of senators in a state
   _____
   _____

8. January 20 _____
   _____
   _____

9. 35 years old, 14 years a resident of the United States, natural-born U.S. citizen _____
   _____
   _____

10. cabinet _____
    _____
    _____

11. 2/3 of the U.S. Senate _____
    _____
    _____

12. treason _____
    _____
    _____

13. the Electoral College _____
    _____
    _____

14. 14 members _____
    _____
    _____

15. simple majority of the Senate
    _____
    _____

Article III – Judicial Department

The men who wrote our Constitution outlined and defined the powers and duties of our court system in Article 3. Although only the most powerful court—the Supreme Court—is clearly named, provision was made for lower courts to be created as needed by Congress and to empower Congress to also determine which cases are to be heard by the various courts within the framework of the judicial system. The main purpose of our courts is to decide how to settle issues when two parties are opposed to each other. The normal procedure is for a judge or jury to hear the arguments and evidence of both sides and then decide which is right, based on the law. Once that decision is made, if a party is found at fault or guilty, the court then decides how the case is to be settled, whether by ordering one party to pay money to the other, or with criminal cases, deciding the punishment. Finally, our courts serve as the vehicle for interpreting our laws. This task is mainly done by the Supreme Court with the lower courts following their precedents.

Article III, Section 1. The judicial power of the United States, shall be vested in one Supreme Court, and in such inferior courts as the Congress may from time to time ordain and establish. The judges, both of the supreme and inferior courts, shall hold their offices during good behavior, and shall, at stated times, receive for their services, a compensation, which shall not be diminished during their continuance in office.

The Court System

The power to make decisions in court cases shall be given to the Supreme Court and to lower courts established by Congress. The judges who oversee these courts shall hold office for life unless found guilty of misconduct. Their salaries cannot be lowered while they are in office. *In this paragraph, Congress was given the power to establish lower courts as needed. Since that time, Congress has indeed eliminated those courts no longer needed and created new ones whenever necessary. The Supreme Court is the most important court and rules over all other courts. Beneath it lie the 11 circuit courts of appeal; and beneath them are found the 96 district courts, which is where a case involving federal law begins. There are also other special courts created by Congress to deal with specific types of cases.*

Article III, Section 2, clause 1. The judicial power shall extend to all cases, in law and equity, arising under this Constitution, the laws of the United States, and treaties made, or which shall be made, under their authority;

to all cases affecting ambassadors, other public ministers and consuls;

to all cases of admiralty and maritime jurisdiction;

to controversies to which the United States shall be a party;

to controversies between two or more states;

[between a state and citizens of another state;]

between citizens of different states,

between citizens of the same state claiming lands under grants of different states, and between a state, or the citizens thereof, and foreign states, [citizens or subjects].

The Power of Federal Courts

The power of the federal courts extends to all cases involving the Constitution, the laws of the United States and treaties made with foreign countries. In addition federal courts cover:

- all cases involving ambassadors of foreign countries

- cases involving ships

- cases in which the U.S. government is one of the parties involved

- cases where one of the states and citizens of another state are involved

- cases between citizens of different states

- cases involving disputes over grants of land

- cases where one of the states and a foreign country or its citizens are the parties involved

- cases where an American citizen and a foreign country or its citizens are the parties involved.

The 11th Amendment removed the power of federal courts from hearing cases between a state and the citizens of another state. While this paragraph gives federal courts the power to hear cases involving the Constitution, it does not clearly define what has come to be known as judicial review—the power to determine whether or not a law made by Congress falls within the framework of the Constitution. This power is one of the checks used by the judicial department over both the legislative and executive branches of our government.

Article III, Section 2, clause 2. In all cases affecting ambassadors, other public ministers and consuls, and those in which a state shall be party, the Supreme Court shall have original jurisdiction. In all the other cases before mentioned, the Supreme Court shall have appellate jurisdiction, both as to law and fact, with such exceptions, and under such regulations as the Congress shall make.

Cases Heard by the Supreme Court

In cases involving foreign ambassadors or states, the Supreme Court has original jurisdiction. Original jurisdiction is defined as the right to hear a case for the first time and make a decision. In all other cases brought before the Supreme Court, it has appellate jurisdiction. Appellate jurisdiction is defined as reviewing a case that has already been heard in a lower court. Congress shall decide the types of cases that can be appealed. *Most federal cases begin in the U.S. District Courts. These courts have only original jurisdiction. Decisions reached by these courts can be appealed to the U. S. Court of Appeals. At this level, the case is reviewed to see if there were any mistakes made in the handling of the case in the District Court that could have affected the decision of the jury. This appellate court does not hear any new evidence. Its task is to review what took place in the District Court. The Supreme Court has both original and appellate jurisdiction. Most of its case load comes from appeals brought from the Court of Appeals, but the Supreme Court decides which cases it will review. If a case is appealed to the Supreme Court from the Appellate and the Supreme Court refuses to hear the case, then the Appellate Court's decision is final. If the Supreme Court does choose to hear the case, then its decision becomes final. There are no appeals beyond the Supreme Court. The Supreme Court must be selective in the cases it hears because it could not possibly review all the cases that are appealed to it. The court chooses various kinds of cases involving points of law that need clarification and interpretation. Their decisions then serve as landmarks for the lower courts to refer to in future similar cases.*

Article III, Section 2, clause 3. The trial of all crimes, except in cases of impeachment, shall be by jury; and such trial shall be held in the state where the said crimes shall have been committed; but when not committed within any state, the trial shall be at such place or places as the Congress may by law have directed.

Article III, Section 3, clause 1. Treason against the United States, shall consist only in levying war against them, or in adhering to their enemies, giving them aid and comfort. No person shall be convicted of treason unless on the testimony of two witnesses to the same overt act, or on confession in open court.

Article III, Section 3, clause 2. The Congress shall have power to declare the punishment of treason, but no attainder of treason shall work corruption of blood or forfeiture except during the life of the person attainted.

Trial by Jury

Anyone accused of committing a crime has a right to a trial by jury, and that trial must be held in the state where the crime was committed. If the crime did not take place in any state, then Congress shall decide where the case will be heard.

Treason

Treason is defined in the Constitution as levying war against the United States or helping its enemies. A person cannot be convicted of treason unless at least two witnesses to the act testify against him or her in court or if the accused confesses to the deed in open court.

Punishment for Treason

Congress shall determine the punishment for treason, but the punishment must not extend to the guilty person's relatives. No corruption of blood means that the family members of the guilty must not suffer for his or her deeds, nor can they have their property taken away.

Original vs. Appellate Jurisdiction

There are two kinds of jurisdiction which a court may have. They are *original* and *appellate*. Original jurisdiction is the power of a court to hear a case for the first time and pass judgment on that case.

Appellate jurisdiction is the power to review a case that has already been heard in a lower court. The decision of the Appellate Court may either uphold the lower court or it may reverse the lower court's decision.

Using what you learned from Article 3 of the Constitution, create a simple diagram showing the structure of the federal court system. Your drawing should show the progressive importance and type of jurisdiction at each level.

Becoming a Federal Judge

1. Most of our public officials are elected by the people they serve. Why do you think the men who wrote the Constitution provided for federal judges to be appointed by the President for a life term?

   _____

   _____

   _____

   _____

2. What problems might occur as a result of judges being appointed for life?

   _____

   _____

   _____

   _____

3. What are the two ways a judge would leave his or her assignment before his or her life ends?

   _____

   _____

   _____

4. What two steps are involved in becoming a federal judge?

   a. _____

   b. _____

Pinpointing Jurisdiction

1. The Supreme Court is the single most powerful judicial force in the United States. Its decisions cannot be overruled. Find out the names, ages, and years of service of each justice currently serving on the Supreme Court.

Name	Age	Years on Court
_____	_____	_____
_____	_____	_____
_____	_____	_____
_____	_____	_____
_____	_____	_____
_____	_____	_____
_____	_____	_____
_____	_____	_____
_____	_____	_____

2. Research news magazines, newspapers, or the Internet to find a recent ruling handed down by the Supreme Court. Analyze the ruling. Write a brief essay and attach the article to your paper. Make sure to include the following:

• the type of jurisdiction

• the focus or point of law that brought the case before the Supreme Court

• the "opinion" or reason cited for the court's eventual decision

• the effect of the decision, i.e., who will be most affected and how

Federal Courts

1. The Supreme Court has both original and appellate jurisdictions. While most of its case load is directed toward ruling on appeals from lower courts (appellate), there are occasions when the court hears a case for the first time. Decide the kind of jurisdiction the Supreme Court has in each of the following cases. Write the word *original* or *appellate* on each line.

   a. _____ A court has decided that teaching is the kind of work where there is no clear relationship between age and ability to do the job; that knowledge and experience can actually increase a person's value in such jobs; that because of this the state of Mississippi cannot force Mavis Petersen to retire from teaching just because she is 65 years old.

   b. _____ Anthony Ray Wilson was convicted of a crime he committed while under the influence of a drug prescribed by his doctor. His lawyer is making a plea before the Supreme Court to overrule his client's prison sentence.

   c. _____ An ambassador to the United States is arrested for breaking into a U.S. military site. When arrested, she is found with copies of several top secret government documents.

2. Assign each of the following cases to the appropriate federal court. Write *U.S. District Court, Circuit Court,* or *Supreme Court.*

   a. _____ A world renowned terrorist is linked to an explosive device that is found in a briefcase on a plane. Fortunately, the bomb was discovered before takeoff and removed without causing any damage or injury. The terrorist is arrested.

   b. _____ The ambassador to the United States from a small Arab nation is arrested for a hit and run incident in which a young girl on a bicycle was seriously injured.

   c. _____ Wilbur Conley was convicted of cheating the U.S. government by failing to report a large portion of his income to the IRS. Wilbur's lawyer claims that some of the evidence used against his client was gained illegally, and he wants to appeal the case.

Checks and Balances

The framers of the Constitution wanted to be certain that no one person or group of persons could ever seize power and control the new American government. To ensure that this never happened, the United States government under the Constitution was divided into three branches: the *legislative,* the *executive* and the *judicial.* This system provides a *balance* of power which allows each branch to *check* the others against abusing their powers.

One example of how this system works is described below:

The executive branch can check the legislative branch by vetoing bills. The legislative branch can check the executive branch by overriding the veto. The judicial branch can check both the legislative and executive branches by declaring laws unconstitutional.

Some other checks and balances are:

Executive over judicial—The President appoints all federal judges.

Legislative over executive—The legislative branch must approve all appointments made by the President. The Senate must approve treaties made by the President, and the legislative branch must investigate certain irregularities in the executive branch (like the uncovering of Watergate).

Legislative over judicial—The legislative branch must approve of the President's choices for judicial appointments (judges).

Legislative over executive and judicial—The legislative branch has the power to impeach and remove from office all important federal officers.

There are other checks and balances in the American government besides those between the three branches of government.

Senate and House of Representatives: The Senate and the House can check each other by rejecting bills passed by the other house. The House has the added check of the sole power to introduce revenue bills.

Checks on the People: A President is not elected directly by the people; only one-third of the Senate is elected at any one time; judges are not elected by the people.

Federalism: Another check is the theory of Federalism. This is a division of power between the national government and the state governments. In many ways, this is a very natural division of power. State affairs are handled by state governments; national affairs are handled by the federal government. The Constitution lists certain specific powers that belong to the federal government. These are called *enumerated powers.* In addition, Congress has the authority to pass laws that are "necessary and proper" in order to fulfill the purposes of the Constitution. Powers under this authority are called *implied powers.*

Since the Constitution does *not* list in detail the powers belonging to the states, there have been many conflicts over their respective powers. The Constitution does say that any "powers not delegated by the Constitution to the federal government are reserved to the states and to the people." These are called *reserve powers.*

The System at Work

Write a letter in each box to show how the right of one branch checks the power of another. The first one has been done for you. Note: Some letters may be used more than once.

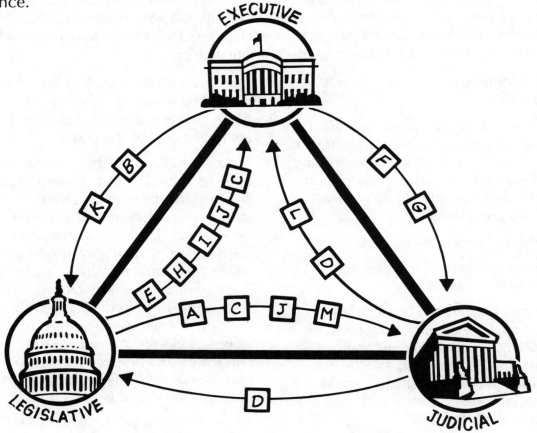

a. Can propose amendments to overrule judicial decisions

b. Can propose bills and call special sessions of the Congress

c. Can refuse to approve judicial appointments

d. Can declare laws unconstitutional

e. Can impeach and remove a President from office

f. Can grant pardons and reprieves

g. Can appoint all federal judges to office

h. Can override a presidential veto

i. Can refuse to ratify foreign treaties

j. Can refuse to approve of presidential appointments

k. Has the power of veto

l. Can declare executive acts unconstitutional

m. Can impeach and remove federal judges

The Checks of Power

In each of the following situations, decide who has the power to check the wrong that is being committed.

1. The President is charged with being responsible for a break-in at the opposing party's headquarters.

   _____

2. Congress and the President approve a law that would prevent certain minorities from receiving tax exemptions which others are entitled to receive.

   _____

3. A federal judge has been accused of accepting large donations from companies which have received some rather favorable rulings from her in the past.

   _____

4. Because the Democrats have an overwhelming majority in both houses, they have decided to pass mass legislation which will help advance the party's goals.

   _____

5. The President is tired of the hundreds of bills that have crossed his desk for action during the past two years. He decides that he will veto all future bills regardless of their nature.

   _____

6. Three days before Congress is scheduled to adjourn, its members decide to deluge the President with approved legislation. Congress hopes that he will hastily sign them into law without careful consideration.

   _____

7. The President would like the Supreme Court to be more conservative in its rulings. In the past year, two justices have left the court, one by death and the other through retirement.

   _____

Judicial Department

Below are some definitions specific to the Judicial Department. On the line, write a word or phrase that best matches each definition.

1. _____ our most powerful court

2. _____ the U.S. court where most federal cases begin

3. _____ the federal court where appeals are heard

4. _____ appoints federal judges to office

5. _____ approves of federal judge appointments

6. _____ the kind of jurisdiction a court has when it hears a case for the first time

7. _____ the kind of jurisdiction a court has when it reviews the action of a lower court

8. _____ the power to determine whether or not a law made by Congress falls within the framework of the Constitution

9. _____ sometimes make the decisions reached in a district court

10. _____ the number of persons who serve on the U.S. Supreme Court

11. _____ to levy war against the United States or help its enemies

12. _____ the number of witnesses required to testify in court against a person charged with treason

13. _____ the terms of office for federal judges

14. _____ the source of rulings in the circuit courts of appeal

15. _____ the vote needed to reach a decision in the Supreme Court

16. _____ the vote needed to reach a decision by the jury in a U.S. District Court criminal trial

17. _____ the steps involved in removing a federal judge

18. _____ the title of the person who sits at the head of the Supreme Court

Article IV – The States and the Federal Government

Once the separation of powers had been assigned and defined among the three branches of government, it became necessary to determine how the states were to interact and relate to each other. That was the purpose of Article 4.

Article IV, Section 1. Full faith and credit shall be given in each state to the public acts, records, and judicial proceedings of every other state. And the Congress may by general laws prescribe the manner in which such acts, records and proceedings shall be proved, and the effect thereof.

Article IV, Section 2, clause 1. The citizens of each state shall be entitled to all privileges and immunities of citizens in the several states.

Article IV, Section 2, clause 2. A person charged in any state with treason, felony, or other crime, who shall flee from justice, and be found in another state, shall on demand of the executive authority of the state from which he fled, be delivered up, to be removed to the state having jurisdiction of the crime.

Article IV, Section 2 clause 3. No person held to service or labor in one state, under the laws thereof, escaping into another, shall, in consequence of any law or regulation therein, be discharged from such service or labor, but shall be delivered up on claim of the party to whom such service or labor may be due.

Full Faith and Credit

All states must respect the laws and court rulings of all other states. Congress shall make rules that will ensure that this happens.

Citizen Rights in Other States

The citizens in each state have the same rights as the citizens of other states.

Extradition

A person charged of committing a crime in one state cannot flee from justice by going to another state. Once captured, he shall be returned to the state in which the crime took place upon request of that state's governor. *This return of a prisoner to another state where a crime was committed is called extradition.*

Dealing with Runaway Slaves

Slaves and indentured servants could not become free men by simply escaping to a free state. Once caught, they were returned to their owners. *Slaves were defined as those forced to do the work of others. The 13th Amendment to the Constitution outlawed slavery. But this clause was placed in Article 4 to ensure that states honored the laws and rules of other states, even though there was a conflict of values over the issues associated with slavery.*

Article IV, Section 3, clause 1. New states may be admitted by the Congress into this union;

but no new state shall be formed or erected within the jurisdiction of any other state;

nor any state be formed by the junction of two or more states, or parts of states, without the consent of the legislatures of the states concerned as well as of the Congress.

Article IV, Section 3, clause 2. The Congress shall have power to dispose of and make all needful rules and regulations respecting the territory or other property belonging to the United States;

and nothing in this Constitution shall be so construed as to prejudice any claims of the United States, or of any particular state.

Article IV, Section 4. The United States shall guarantee to every state in this Union a republican form of government, and shall protect each of them against invasion; and on application of the legislature, or of the executive (when the legislature cannot be convened) against domestic violence.

How New States Enter the Union

New states are admitted to the Union by Congress, but no state may be divided into other states without the approval of the states involved and Congress. In cases where two existing states want to unite to become a single state, both Congress and the states involved must agree to the union. *Two states have been formed by dividing already existing states, but no states have been formed by uniting already existing states.*

Treatment of Territories

Congress shall have the power to sell or to give away land belonging to the United States. Congress shall also make laws to govern the territories. Nothing in the Constitution shall be interpreted to favor one state over another, or to favor a state in a disputed land claim. *The purpose of this paragraph was to give the Congress firm control over all U.S. territories. There was also some concern that some states might feel the Constitution would favor certain states. This paragraph was written to assure them this would not happen.*

Guarantees to All the States

The United States guarantees a republican form of government to every state in the Union. It shall also protect each state from invasion. Upon request by a state legislature or its chief executive, it will also help to stop riots within the state. *This paragraph guarantees a republican form of government to every state. This is a government where the people vote for their choices for those they wish to make the laws and enforce them.*

Full Faith and Credit Clause

1. The full faith and credit clause (Article 4, Section 1) is one of the most important statements made in the Constitution. Refer back to the reasons for the failure of the Articles of Confederation. Explain why this paragraph helped the states avoid those problems.

_____

_____

_____

_____

2. In keeping with Article 4, Section 3, clause 1, Congress has formed two new states by dividing existing states. Find out which two states were created this way and describe the historical incidents that led to their creation.

_____

_____

_____

_____

3. Article 4, Section 4 guarantees a republican form of government. Find out the differences between a true democracy and a republican form of government and tell why a true democracy would not be possible in the United States.

_____

_____

_____

_____

Article V – Amending the Constitution

The Constitution was designed to have a great deal of flexibility. The framers knew that if the document were to withstand the test of time, they would have to provide a reasonable way to change or add to it, as society itself would change over the generations. Article 5 provides two plans.

Article V. The Congress, whenever two-thirds of both houses shall deem it necessary, shall propose amendments to this Constitution, or, on the application of the legislatures of two-thirds of the several states, shall call a convention for proposing amendments, which, in either case, shall be valid to all intents and purposes, as part of this Constitution, when ratified by the legislatures of three-fourths of the several states, or by conventions in three-fourths thereof, as the one or the other mode of ratification may be proposed by the Congress;

provided [that no amendment which may be made prior to the year one thousand eight hundred and eight shall in any matter affect the first and fourth clauses in the ninth section of the first article; and]

that no state, without its consent, shall be deprived of its equal suffrage in the Senate.

Procedures for Amending the Constitution

Amendments can be proposed in either of two ways. Two-thirds of both houses of Congress may propose a change, or an amendment may be proposed by having two-thirds of the state legislatures call for a special convention that will propose the amendment. Once an amendment is officially proposed, it must then be ratified to become a valid part of the Constitution. This ratification can occur in either of the following ways: the state legislatures in three-fourths of the states must vote for approval, or special conventions in three-fourths of the states can vote for approval. No amendment made prior to the year 1808 can affect the slave trade or provide for a different way of figuring taxes. No state without its consent can have its number of senators decreased. *The framers of the Constitution intentionally made it difficult for an amendment to be ratified. They wanted enough flexibility to change the Constitution if change was necessary; but such change could not be accomplished without a great deal of effort and a genuine agreement among most of the people.*

☆ Amending the Constitution ☆

Use the encyclopedia, periodicals, or the Internet to research answers to these questions. You might need to write your answers on a separate paper.

1. How many amendments have been made to the original Constitution?

_____

2. How many of those were proposed by Congress, and how many were proposed through special convention?

_____

3. How many of the amendments were ratified by the state legislatures and how many were ratified by conventions held in the states?

_____

4. Once an amendment to the Constitution has been officially proposed, how long does it have until it must either be adopted as a part of the Constitution (by receiving proper ratification) or dropped (for not receiving the required approval).

_____

5. What is the number of states required to approve an amendment to the Constitution?

_____

6. Research the battle over the Equal Rights Amendment of the 1970s and early 80s. What were the issues at stake? What was the eventual outcome?

_____

7. What amendment to the Constitution would you propose? On another sheet of paper, write a persuasive essay convincing others to support your proposed amendment.

Article VI – General Provisions

With all of the powers defined, the relationship between the states and the federal government established, and the rules set forth for amending the Constitution, only a few general statements remained to be stated.

Article VI, clause 1. All debts contracted and engagements entered into, before the adoption of this Constitution, shall be as valid against the United States under this Constitution, as under the Confederation.

Article VI, clause 2. This Constitution, and the laws of the United States which shall be made in pursuance thereof; and all treaties made, or which shall be made, under the authority of the United States, shall be the supreme law of the land; and the judges in every state shall be bound thereby, anything in the Constitution or laws of any state to the contrary notwithstanding.

Article VI, clause 3. The senators and representatives before mentioned, and the members of the several state legislatures, and all executive and judicial officers, both of the United States and of the several states, shall be bound by oath or affirmation, to support this Constitution; but no religious test shall ever be required as a qualification to any office or public trust under the United States.

General Provisions

All debts and treaties entered into prior to the adoption of the Constitution shall be considered valid and will be honored by the United States.

This Constitution shall be the supreme law of the land. All laws made by Congress and all treaties entered into by the United States shall be made in accordance with its rules and provisions, and all state judges must follow its guidelines. If they find laws in their states which contradict the Constitution, they must rule in favor of the Constitution.

All members of Congress, the various state legislatures plus all officers of the executive and judicial departments, both at the federal and state levels are required to affirm by oath their promise to uphold and support the Constitution. But no official or public employee can ever be subjected to a religious test as a condition of his or her employment.

General Provisions

1. What message were the framers of the Constitution announcing to the rest of the world in the first paragraph of Article 6? Why was this an important statement?

   _____

   _____

   _____

   _____

2. If there is ever a conflict between a state law and a federal law that falls within the framework of the Constitution, which takes precedence? Why is this an important distinction to make? How did this philosophy differ from the Articles of Confederation?

   _____

   _____

   _____

   _____

   _____

3. Why do you think the writers of the Constitution insisted that no religious test be given as a condition of employment for any public employee?

   _____

   _____

   _____

   _____

With the framework well-established and all the specifics in place, the only task that remained was to determine how the Constitution would be approved by the states it would serve. There had been many battles through the long months of hammering out the Constitution, and the members of the Convention wanted to make certain their work was adopted, so they were very careful in the rules they set up for ratification.

Article VII. The ratification of the conventions of nine states, shall be sufficient for the establishment of this Constitution between the states so ratifying the same.

Done in convention by the unanimous consent of the states present the seventeenth day of September in the year of our Lord one thousand seven hundred and eighty-seven and of the independence of the United States of America the twelfth. In witness whereof we have hereunto subscribed our names.

Ratification

The ratification of the Constitution shall be considered sufficient whenever conventions in nine of the states have approved. The Constitution was officially signed on September 17, 1787, the twelfth year after our independence, by the unanimous consent of the twelve states present. In witness to this, these were the names of those who signed. *The writers called for conventions to be held in the states rather than allowing the state legislatures to decide whether or not their states would ratify the Constitution. They did this because they felt conventions called for the specific purpose of ratification would be more likely to approve.*

Ratification

Article VII

1. How many states were represented at the Constitutional Convention? _____

2. Which state was not represented at the Constitutional Convention?

   _____

3. How many signatures are there on the original document? _____

4. Which state had the most number of signatures on the original Constitution?

   _____

5. What was the requirement established by the Constitutional Convention for ratifying the new Constitution?

   _____

6. Which state was the first to ratify the Constitution?

   _____

7. How long did it take for the Constitution to receive the necessary approval votes for ratification? When did the Constitution go into effect?

   _____

   _____

8. Some states took longer to ratify the Constitution than others? Why do you think this might have happened?

   _____

   _____

Review Articles IV–VII

Show what you know about Articles 4–7. Refer to your research notes and, the text of the Constitution to help. Write a word or phrase that best fits with the statement given.

1. _____ transferring an accused criminal back to the state where a crime was committed

2. _____ the number of states needed to ratify the Constitution

3. _____ the article where the full faith and credit clause is found

4. _____ the branch that holds the power to admit new states into the Union

5. _____ the two states that were created by dividing existing states

6. _____ the body that holds the power to govern all U.S. territories

7. _____ the number of signatures on the original Constitution

8. _____ the date when the Constitution was signed

9. _____ the number of states needed to ratify an amendment to the Constitution

10. _____ the number of amendments to the Constitution

11. _____ the state not represented when the Constitution was signed

12. _____ the two methods of proposing a constitutional amendment

13. _____ the two methods of ratifying a constitutional amendment

14. _____ the authority for deciding the method used in ratifying an amendment

15. _____ the Supreme Law of the Land

16. _____ the year the Constitution took effect

17. _____ It defines a political society in which the people elect their leaders who make the laws and enforce them.

18. _____ If a state is having problems with domestic violence (riots), this authority can ask for federal assistance to restore peace.

Bill of Rights

The men who wrote the original Constitution did not think it was necessary to list the individual rights of the people. They assumed that because the various state constitutions contained lists of individual rights, then it should not be necessary to place them in the U.S. Constitution. When copies of the new Constitution were dispatched to the states and the people for a "first look," they found out differently.

There was an overwhelming insistence among the people that an assurance of the individual rights of men and women should be spelled out very clearly in the Constitution. Such was the condition under which several of the state conventions ratified the Constitution. They would ratify the document only if a bill of rights would be added. Congress was quick to comply.

The Constitution went into effect in 1789. In that same year, it reviewed more than twenty amendments suggested by the ratifying convention. Congress pared the list down to twelve, which were submitted to the states to be ratified. Ten of them were approved and became part of the Constitution by 1791.

Because they followed so soon after the original document, they are looked at historically as almost being a part of the original document. But they clearly point to one of the first major uses of the Constitution as the framework of the American nation—namely the process involved in changing it (amending) to suit the needs of the people. These first ten amendments also point to the power of the people themselves to make certain that their own liberties were not overlooked.

The new Constitution had clearly defined the power of the federal government, and it had established the supremacy of the federal government over any and all state governments. The people wanted their rights protected, too. They got their wish in the form of the first ten amendments, known as the Bill of Rights.

Amendment I

Congress shall make no law respecting an establishment of religion, or prohibiting the free exercise thereof;

or abridging the freedom of speech, or of the press;

or the right of the people peaceably to assemble, and to petition the government for a redress of grievances.

The Five Freedoms

Congress can make no law that establishes an official religion, nor can it pass laws that prohibit people from following any religion they choose, as long as the practices of the religion do not violate any of our other laws;

nor can Congress pass laws that prohibit people from speaking and writing their thoughts;

nor can Congress pass laws that will prevent people from gathering together peacefully to discuss their government and appeal to it to correct any wrong they feel may have been done.

There are actually five freedoms very precious to the people pointed out in this 1st Amendment. They are freedom of religion, speech, press, assembly, and petition. This amendment intended to provide the people with the freedoms necessary for self-expression; but these freedoms have some limitations and restrictions. The courts must protect people from pursuing their own self-interests to the point of bringing harm to other people, or in some way violating their own personal rights. The letter of the law is unclear in some situations, and it takes a court to decide whether or not personal rights have been violated.

Amendment II

A well-regulated militia, being necessary to the security of a free state, the right of the people to keep and bear arms shall not be infringed.

Amendment III

No soldier shall, in time of peace be quartered in any house, without the consent of the owner, nor in time of war, but in a manner to be prescribed by law.

Amendment IV

The right of the people to be secure in their persons, houses, papers and effects, against unreasonable searches and seizures, shall not be violated, and no warrants shall issue, but upon probable cause, supported by oath or affirmation, and particularly describing the place to be searched, and the persons or things to be seized.

The Right to Bear Arms

Because it is necessary to maintain a militia of men ready to defend the country, Congress does not have the right to keep people from owning and carrying guns. This amendment continues to generate controversy in its interpretation.

Quartering Soldiers

No soldier, during peacetime, can be forced into the homes of private citizens. And during war, soldiers can be placed in private homes only in a manner as prescribed by Congress.

Search and Seizure

Unless a proper search warrant has been authorized, a person has a right to protect his or her own person, home, papers, and personal effects. A search warrant can only be issued through a court of law if proper explanation of why the search needs to be made has been provided. That explanation must include the place to be searched, the reason for the search and exactly who or what is expected to be found. *The people insisted on this protection for themselves and their property to prevent the police and the military from unnecessarily invading their property. Many people had been subjected to unreasonable searches while under the rule of England. They did not want this to be part of the new Constitution. If a search warrant is issued, the judge must be presented with solid evidence that there is good cause for issuing one.*

Amendment V

No person shall be held to answer for a capital, or otherwise infamous crime, unless on a presentment or indictment of a grand jury, except in cases arising in the land or naval forces, or in the militia, when in actual service in time of war or public danger;

nor shall any person be subject for the same offense to be twice put in jeopardy of life or limb;

nor shall be compelled in any criminal case to be a witness against himself,

nor be deprived of life, liberty, or property, without due process of law;

nor shall private property be taken for public use without just compensation.

Rights of the Accused in Court

No person shall be tried for a serious criminal act unless he or she has first been presented an indictment by a grand jury, except in cases involving members of the military during times of war or public danger. *An indictment is a formal charge that accuses a person of having committed a crime. That indictment is issued by a grand jury which examines the evidence against the accused to determine whether or not there will even be a trial. The grand jury is usually composed of 16 to 23 persons. If a simple majority of its members agree that there is enough evidence against the accused, an indictment is issued and the guilt or innocence of that accused person will be determined in a court of law by a petit jury, where both sides are heard.*

Nor shall any person be subjected to double jeopardy. *The double jeopardy clause refers to the fact that a person cannot be tried a second time for a crime if he or she was found not guilty during an earlier trial.*

Nor shall anyone be forced to say anything in court that could lead to his or her conviction;

nor can anyone be deprived of life, liberty, or property without due process of law. *Due process of law is the sum total of the letter of the law as viewed by the courts. This statement is further assurance that the accused will be given a fair trial and none of his personal effects will be taken unfairly from him.*

Nor can private property be taken for public use without the government paying a fair price for it. *The government does indeed have the right to take private land for public use. That right is called eminent domain. But if the courts do rule in favor of public use, then the government must pay the landowner a fair price for it.*

Amendment VI

In all criminal prosecutions, the accused shall enjoy the right to a speedy and public trial, by an impartial jury of the state and district wherein the crime shall have been committed, which district shall have been previously ascertained by law, and to be informed of the nature and cause of the accusation;

to be confronted with the witnesses against him;

to have compulsory process for obtaining witnesses in his favor, and to have the assistance of counsel for his defense.

Additional Rights in Court

Anyone accused of committing a crime has a right to a speedy and public trial. The guilt or innocence of the accused shall be determined by an impartial jury made up of citizens that live in the state and district where the crime was committed. The accused must be given proper notification of the charge for which he or she is being tried.

The accused has the right to be present in court and to see those who are witnesses against him or her.

The accused also has the right to call witnesses to court to testify in his or her behalf. Even if they do not wish to volunteer to appear in court, the witnesses can be forced to attend and testify through a court order called a *subpoena*. The accused also has a right to be properly defended during his or her trial. If he or she cannot afford an attorney, the court will appoint one to serve in his or her behalf.

Amendment VII

In suits at common law, where the value in controversy shall exceed twenty dollars, the right of a trial by jury shall be preserved, and no fact tried by a jury, shall be otherwise reexamined in any court of the United States, than according to the rules of the common law.

Jury Trials

When there is a dispute over property where the value exceeds twenty dollars, either party can insist that a jury decide the issue. If the case is appealed to a higher court, that court must render a decision based upon the facts presented in that specific case. *Both parties may also agree to present their case before a judge and allow the judge to make the decision. This cuts down on the cost and helps to avoid the backlog of cases in the court system.*

Amendment VIII

Excessive bail shall not be required, nor excessive fines imposed, nor cruel and unusual punishments inflicted.

Excessive Bail and Punishment

Excessive *bail* shall not be allowed. The punishments assessed by courts against those found guilty of committing crimes cannot be excessive nor can they be cruel or unusual. *Bail is the amount of money the court requires the accused to pay to ensure that he or she will show up for trial. If the bail is met, the accused is allowed to go free until the trial. The amount of bail is determined by a judge. This amendment also insists that courts make the punishment suit the crime that has been committed. Excessive punishments are outlawed and the cruel and unusual punishments of early New England were also ruled out.*

Amendment IX

The enumeration in the Constitution, of certain rights, shall not be construed to deny or disparage others retained by the people.

Rights of the People

The listing of the specific personal rights of the people already found in the Constitution does not mean that people do not have other rights. Those other rights may also be just as important as those listed. *Those who wrote the bill of rights soon realized that they could not list every single right afforded to individuals. The 9th Amendment is designed to cover all those not listed. Some are quite obvious; some are not so obvious and have led to challenges in court.*

Amendment X

The powers not delegated to the United States by the Constitution, nor prohibited by it to the states, are reserved to the states respectively, or to the people.

Rights of the States

Those powers not specifically set aside for the federal government nor denied the states and the people are reserved for the states and the people. *Here again is another statement assuring those who would later interpret the Constitution that both the states and the people have rights in addition to those that appear in the Constitution.*

Bill of Rights

Amendment I: The Five Freedoms

1. List the five freedoms granted in the 1st Amendment.

   a. _____

   b. _____

   c. _____

   d. _____

   e. _____

2. The 1st Amendment says people may say or write anything they want. There are, however, some limitations placed on this precious freedom. Describe two situations where someone might be restricted from exercising this freedom completely.

   _____

3. What are the possible consequences people risk when they refuse to respect the limits placed on freedom of speech and freedom of the press?

   _____

4. When would restrictions be placed upon a person's freedom to worship in whatever manner he or she chooses?

   _____

5. What is the difference between the right to assemble and the right to petition?

   _____

Amendment II: Right to Bear Arms

6. The 2nd Amendment established the right of a state to have a militia. What did it say about the right of private individuals to own weapons?

   _____

7. Describe some of the restrictions placed on citizens' constitutional right "to bear arms." Why have restrictions been placed on this right?

   _____

Amendment III: Quartering Soldiers

8. During peacetime, no soldier shall be quartered in a house without the consent of the owner. Where did this idea come from?

_____

_____

Amendment IV: Search and Seizure

9. Under the 4th Amendment, what items are protected from unwarranted searches?

_____

_____

10. What information must be contained in an authorized search warrant?

_____

_____

Amendment V: Rights of the Accused in Court

11. What is the difference between a capital crime and an infamous crime?

_____

_____

12. No person can be punished for a capital crime or for an infamous crime without first having been indicted by a grand jury. What is an indictment?

_____

_____

13. What is a grand jury and what does it do?

_____

14. How many people usually serve on a grand jury?

_____

15. What happens after the grand jury issues an indictment?

_____

16. The 5th Amendment states that a person shall not be placed in "double jeopardy." What does that mean?

   _____

   _____

17. You have probably heard the familiar phrase, "I plead the fifth." What specific part of the 5th Amendment is a defendant referring to when he or she says these words?

   _____

18. No person may have life, liberty, or property taken from him or her without due process of law. What does the phrase *due process of law* mean?

   _____

Amendment VI: Additional Rights in Court

19. In all cases of criminal prosecution, the accused shall have the right to a speedy and public trial. What does the 6th Amendment say about where that trial should be held?

   _____

20. The accused has the right to be judged by a jury of 12 unbiased persons and must be completely informed of all existing rights. One of those rights is to confront, face to face, those who testify against him or her. Why do you think this right is guaranteed?

   _____

21. What do we call the court order that forces witnesses for the accused to appear and testify in court whether they want to or not?

   _____

Amendment VII: Jury Trials

22. What is the minimum dollar amount over which a common lawsuit can be filed?

   _____

23. The decision of the jury shall be final except under either of these two circumstances:

   a. _____

   b. _____

Amendment VIII: Excessive Bail and Punishment

24. What is bail?

_____

25. Research the history of early colonial America and find some examples of cruel and unusual punishment which the framers of the Constitution might have had in mind when they wrote the 8th Amendment.

_____

26. The Supreme Court has the final word in deciding what is cruel or excessive. On June 29, 1972, the Supreme Court ruled that capital punishment was unconstitutional on the grounds that it was being administered unfairly. They decided the manner in which it was being administered was in and of itself cruel and excessive, and violated the 8th Amendment. Since that time, the Supreme Court has reversed that decision. As long as the punishment is administered fairly to all, it is no longer considered cruel nor excessive. Hundreds of executions have been carried out in the United States. What is your own opinion of capital punishment? Support your statement with at least two examples.

_____

_____

Amendment IX: Rights of the People

27. The 9th Amendment says that the Constitution has given us all certain rights, but all of those rights cannot be listed. Just because a right is not listed in the Constitution does not mean that it does not exist. Give three examples of rights people have that are not listed.

_____

28. How is the 9th Amendment similar to Article 1, Section 8, clause 18?

_____

Amendment X: Rights of the States

29. Any powers not specifically given to the federal government in the Constitution are given to whom?

_____

_____

Our Living Bill of Rights

Decide which of the first ten amendments applies in each case below and explain the point of law that is the issue.

1. The Coalition for a Peaceful World planned a rally in front of the U.S. Capitol Building to protest the new budget prepared by the President and Congress. Their main concern was a large increase in defense spending to build a new missile defense system. The CPW has a reputation for being somewhat radical, and trouble sometimes follows. The group has registered properly with the authorities; however, armed police will still be present.

   _____

   _____

   _____

2. Antonio Morales had been arrested many times for drug dealing. Recently, the police suspected Antonio of organizing a sophisticated drug distribution system. The police secured a search warrant that allowed them to search for drugs in Antonio's home. They found no drugs; however, they did find hundreds of brand new CD players with the serial numbers scratched out.

   _____

   _____

   _____

3. Lana Miles was very lucky the day she picked the six winning lotto numbers. She will receive $250,000 a year for the next twenty years. Lana did not really like her job at the carpet mill, so the following day she went into work and quit her job.

   _____

   _____

   _____

4. Two young men decided to steal an elderly woman's purse. The woman was able to identify her attackers and police arrested them the next day. They were convicted of theft and sentenced to two years in jail.

_____

_____

_____

_____

_____

5. A riot erupted in Seattle, Washington. The National Guard was called in to stop the violence and restore peace. Unfortunately, the National Guard had no facilities in the area to house or feed the troops. The residents of Seattle were forced to provide food and shelter for the weary troops.

_____

_____

_____

_____

6. Jason Cunningham is on trial for breaking and entering. The district attorney believes she has enough circumstantial evidence to convict Jason. Jason claims he could not have broken into that home that night because he and two friends were robbing a liquor store in another county at that time. The two friends do not want to cooperate with Jason's lawyer for fear of getting themselves in trouble.

_____

_____

_____

_____

7. A well-known actor was put on trial for murdering his producer in a contract dispute. A jury found the actor not guilty of the crime. Six months later, the police discovered new evidence that proved, without a doubt, the actor had murdered the producer.

_____

_____

_____

_____

8. Kiana Jones lives in a great apartment close to her work in Chicago. There have been seven robberies in her apartment building this year alone. Kiana wants to buy a handgun to protect herself against any intruders.

_____

_____

_____

_____

9. Tomas Chavez bought the property next to Matt Wong six months ago. Tomas had the property surveyed and found that a row of oak trees between the two properties are actually on his land. Tomas wants to cut down the trees and sell the wood. Matt enjoys the trees and feels they provide privacy for his home. Tomas filed a lawsuit against Matt and requested a jury trial to settle the matter.

_____

_____

_____

_____

10. The state of Georgia decided to reorganize its public education system.

_____

_____

_____

_____

Amendment XI

The judicial power of the United States shall not be construed to extend to any suit in law or equity, commenced or prosecuted against one of the United States by citizens of another state, or by citizens or subjects of any foreign state.

Cases Against the States

Private citizens of different states or of foreign countries cannot sue a state in federal court. *Many people felt that allowing such cases to be heard in federal courts as provided in the original Constitution under Article 3 gave the central government too much power.*

Prelude to Amendment XII

The framers of the Constitution created a simple method for electing the President and vice president: the candidate who won the most electoral votes would become President; the candidate with the second greatest number of electoral votes would be vice president. This plan worked until political parties began to emerge.

In the election of 1796, John Adams, who was a Federalist, was elected President and Thomas Jefferson, a Republican, was elected vice president. These two men, who were supposed to be working together, were from entirely different political backgrounds and had conflicting political views.

But the election of 1800 magnified the problem. The Federalists supported John Adams for President and Charles Pinckney for vice president, and the Republicans supported Thomas Jefferson for President and Aaron Burr for vice president. Both Jefferson and Burr ended up with 71 electoral votes, Adams received 65 and Pinckney received 64. Since

no candidate had a majority, the election had to be decided in the House of Representatives. Each state would get one vote.

The Federalist party was not as strong as the Republican party and knew they could not win, but they could prevent someone else from winning. The House of Representatives voted 35 times and each vote ended in a tie. On the thirty-sixth ballot the Federalists gave in and abstained from voting to allow Jefferson to win the election. Such tactics made it quite clear that a new method for electing the President was needed and work began on the 12th Amendment.

Amendment XII

The electors shall meet in their respective states and vote by ballot for President and vice president, one of whom, at least, shall not be an inhabitant of the same state with themselves; they shall name in their ballots the person voted for as President, and in distinct ballots the person voted for as vice president, and they shall make distinct lists of all persons voted for as President, and of all persons voted for as vice president, and of the number of votes for each, which lists they shall sign and certify, and transmit sealed to the seat of the government of the United States, directed to the president of the Senate;

the president of the Senate shall, in the presence of the Senate and House of Representatives, open all the certificates and the votes shall then be counted;

the person having the greatest number of votes for President, shall be the President, if such number be a majority of the whole number of electors appointed; and if no person have such majority, then from the persons having the highest numbers not exceeding three on the list of those voted for as President, the House of Representatives shall choose immediately, by ballot, the President. But in choosing the President, the votes shall be taken by states, the representation from each state having one vote; a quorum for this purpose shall consist of a member or members from two-thirds of the states, and a majority of all the states shall be necessary to a choice.

Electing the President

The electors shall meet in their respective states and cast separate votes for the President and the vice president. At least one of the candidates they vote for must live in another state. The electors then make a list of all those who received votes for President and another list of those who won votes for vice president. They tally up the totals and send both lists to the president of the Senate.

In the presence of both houses of Congress, the president of the Senate opens the votes from each state and tallies the votes.

The person with the most votes for President becomes the President. If no one has a majority, then the House of Representatives shall elect the President from a list of no more than three candidates. In this case, each state has only one vote and there must be at least two-thirds of the states represented when this election takes place. The candidate who has the greatest number of votes shall become President.

And if the House of Representatives shall not choose a President whenever the right of choice shall devolve upon them, [before the fourth day of March next following,] then the vice president shall act as President, as in the case of the death or other constitutional disability of the President.

The person having the greatest number of votes as vice president, shall be the vice president, if such number be a majority of the whole number of electors appointed, and if no person have a majority, then from the two highest numbers on the list, the Senate shall choose the vice president; a quorum for the purpose shall consist of two-thirds of the whole number of senators, and a majority of the whole number shall be necessary to a choice.

But no person constitutionally ineligible to the office of the President shall be eligible to that of vice president of the United States.

If the House of Representatives should fail to choose a President by March 4 (the date when the newly elected President is supposed to assume his office), then the vice president shall act as President. *This part of the amendment was later changed by the 20th Amendment.*

The candidate for vice president with the greatest number of electoral votes for vice president shall become the vice president. But if that candidate does not have a simple majority of all electors, then the vice president shall be chosen by the Senate. The Senate chooses between the two candidates who had the greatest number of electoral votes. Two-thirds of the senators must be present when the vote is taken and the candidate who wins must have a simple majority vote of all the senators.

No person constitutionally ineligible to become President shall be eligible to become vice president either.

The Birth of Political Parties

Article 2 clearly spells out that the President and the vice president shall be elected by the Electoral College made up of electors from each state. The number of electors a state has is dependent upon its population, as each state has as many electors as it has representatives plus two (number of senators). When people vote in a presidential election, they are actually casting their votes for the electors pledged to the candidate of their choice.

Under the original Constitution, there was no distinction between the candidates who ran for President and those who ran for vice president. Each elector voted for two people from the list of candidates. The person with the highest total became President and the runner-up became the vice president.

When George Washington was elected President, he was elected unanimously. There were sixty-nine electors and they all voted for him. John Adams had the second highest total of the men on the list, so he became vice president. There weren't any political campaigns because there weren't any political parties.

Political parties emerge when a significant number of people have the same philosophy and a number of common goals. Such was the case in America. Alexander Hamilton and Thomas Jefferson were chosen by Washington to serve in his cabinet, but they had conflicting political views. Hamilton believed in a strong central government and wanted a loose interpretation of the Constitution that gave Congress, the President, and the courts the latitude to make the decisions that needed to be made. Jefferson believed in the power of the state and local authorities to make their own decisions. He believed it was necessary to restrict the power of the federal government and enforce a strict interpretation of the Constitution. Jefferson's followers became known as the Democratic-Republicans (later, Republicans). Hamilton's supporters were called Federalists.

By the election of 1792, the difference between the political parties was much stronger. Washington was again elected unanimously, but the race for vice president between John Adams (a Federalist) and George Clinton (a Democratic-Republican) was close. When Washington chose not to run for a third term in 1796, the stage was set for the true entry of party politics. The Federalists ran Adams and Thomas Pinckney. The Republicans ran Jefferson and Aaron Burr. It was expected that the electors would support both candidates from their own parties. In the end it was Adams, the Federalist, who became President, and Jefferson, the Republican, who became vice president.

In 1800, Jefferson and Adams again opposed each other, and Burr was running against Pinckney for vice president. This time the electors were very much pledged to their party's candidates. All 73 of the Republican electors voted for both Jefferson and Burr, which resulted in a tie. In the event of a tie, the President was to be elected by the House of Representatives. The House of Representatives, which was controlled by Federalists, voted 35 times. Each vote ended in a tie. The Federalist party leader, Alexander Hamilton, preferred Jefferson to Burr, so he used his influence on the thirty-sixth ballot to help Jefferson win. The election showed that political parties and party loyalty would drastically influence the method of electing our President. The 12th Amendment provided new guidelines for electing the President and vice president.

The Birth of Political Parties

1. Describe the pros and cons of having a President from one party and a vice president from another party.

    _____

    _____

    _____

    _____

2. How did the emergence of political parties change the method of electing the President?

    _____

    _____

    _____

    _____

3. Find out how Aaron Burr expressed his displeasure over the support Alexander Hamilton gave to Thomas Jefferson in the election of 1800.

    _____

    _____

    _____

    _____

4. Research the basic philosophies of the two major political parties today and briefly describe their differences.

    _____

    _____

    _____

    _____

Amendments XI and XII

1. What does the 11th amendment say about cases filed by private citizens against states?

   _____

2. Why did Congress propose the 11th Amendment?

   _____

3. Use the chart below to show how the 12th Amendment changed the method for electing the President and vice president.

	As Defined in Article 2	Under the 12th Amendment
Who actually elects the President?		
Who chooses the electors?		
What is the required vote to win the presidency?		
How is the vice president elected?		

Election Day

The procedure for presidential elections today has each major party presenting a ticket that includes both a presidential candidate and a vice-presidential candidate. The two run as a team. When the people vote, they make their choice from the Democratic presidential candidate and vice-presidential candidate, the Republican presidential candidate and vice-presidential candidate, or a third party's presidential candidate and vice-presidential candidate. People cannot vote for a presidential candidate from one party and a vice-presidential candidate from another party. But as you learned earlier, the people do not directly elect the President and vice president. They are elected by the Electoral College, which is made up of all the electors from all the states. Each state has the same number of electors as it has representatives plus senators. For example, a state with 24 representatives would be entitled to 26 electoral votes (24, its number of representatives, plus 2, its number of senators). That state's major political parties would each choose 26 electors. The people chosen to serve as electors are usually strong party members who have devoted many hours of service.

On election day, the people then decide which set of candidates they prefer. This is called the popular vote. The team of candidates with the most popular votes in the state wins all of the electors in that state. In most states, regardless of how close the popular vote is, the winner gets all the electoral votes. By the end of election night, it is usually known which candidate has won the most electoral votes and thus the presidency. Several weeks later, the winning set of electors in each state meets in their respective state capitals and goes through the formality of casting their votes for the President and vice president.

Election Day

1. Summarize the process of electing the President and vice president.

    _____

    _____

2. Refer to the electoral map of the United States you created on page 66. What is the total number of electoral votes in all of the United States?

    _____

3. What is the number of electoral votes a candidate must have to win the election?

    _____

4. Why is it good political strategy for candidates to spend much of their time and money campaigning in the states that have the most electoral votes?

    _____

    _____

5. List in descending order the ten states that have the most electoral votes and the number each of these states has. How many total electoral votes are represented by these ten states?

    _____   _____   _____

    _____   _____   _____

    _____   _____   _____

    _____

6. Explain why three electoral votes is the smallest number any state may have.

    _____

    _____

In the Wake of War

The Amendments 13, 14, and 15 deal with slavery and the treatment of former slaves. Throughout the early history of America, there had been debate and disagreement over the institution of slavery. When the issue was addressed at the Constitutional Convention, there was so much disagreement that it was questionable as to whether there would even be a Constitution.

Compromise and postponement resolved the issue temporarily. However, the issue of slavery never disappeared and eventually the nation went to war with itself. Hundreds of thousands of lives were lost, families were broken, and much of the South was virtually destroyed in the Civil War. The end result, however, was that the slaves were set free. These amendments provided the constitutional groundwork for healing the nation.

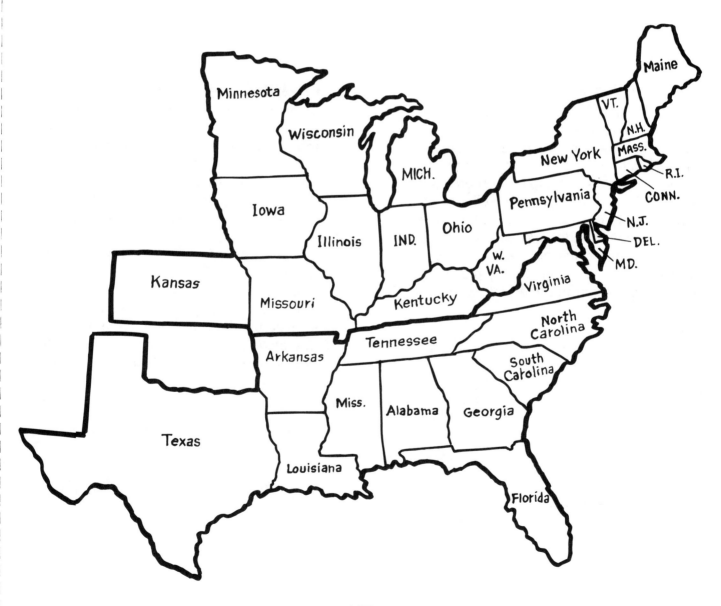

Amendment XIII

Section 1. Neither slavery nor involuntary servitude, except as a punishment for crime whereof the party shall have been duly convicted, shall exist within the United States, or any place subject to their jurisdiction.

Section 2. Congress shall have power to enforce this article by appropriate legislation.

Amendment XIV

Section 1. All persons born or naturalized in the United States, and subject to the jurisdiction thereof, are citizens of the United States and of the state wherein they reside. No state shall make or enforce any law which shall abridge the privileges or immunities of citizens of the United States; nor shall any state deprive any person of life, liberty, or property, without due process of law; nor deny to any person within its jurisdiction the equal protection of the laws.

The Abolition of Slavery

Slavery shall no longer be allowed in the United States or in any land under its jurisdiction. No one may be forced to do the work of another unless the courts decree such work as punishment for committing a crime. *Lincoln's Emancipation Proclamation technically freed all the slaves in the states that had left the Union and joined the Confederacy. Many slave owners had already freed their slaves during the war, but this constitutional amendment made it official that all practices associated with slavery would be forever abolished in the United States.*

Congress shall have the power to make laws that will make this amendment effective.

Former Slaves Made Citizens

All people who are either born here or become naturalized in the United States and are subject to its laws are citizens of the United States. Such citizens are also citizens of the states in which they live, and the states cannot make or enforce laws that may deprive these people of enjoying their rights as U.S. citizens. States cannot take away people's lives, their liberty, or their property without due process of law. People who live in any of our states are entitled to the same protection and benefits enjoyed by all others who live in that state. *This section is cited often in cases filed by those who feel they are being discriminated against.*

Section 2. Representatives shall be apportioned among the several states according to their respective numbers, counting the whole number of persons in each state, [excluding Indians not taxed]. But when the right to vote at any election for the choice of electors for President and vice president of the United States, representatives in Congress, the executive and judicial officers of a state, or the members of the legislature thereof, is denied to any of the male inhabitants of such state, being twenty-one years of age, and citizens of the United States, or in any way abridged, except for participation in rebellion, or other crime, the basis of representation therein shall be reduced in the proportion which the number of such male citizens shall bear to the whole number of male citizens twenty-one years of age in such state.

The number of representatives in the House of Representatives for each state shall be based on a count of all the people in that state except the untaxed Indians. Any state that tries to keep male citizens, who are over twenty-one years of age and who have not been convicted of a crime, from voting in presidential elections shall have their representation in Congress cut proportionately. *This paragraph totally changed the "three-fifths" clause found in Article 1, Section 2, and it intended to force states to grant voting rights to men who had been former slaves. There was a great deal of prejudice and discrimination in the South, and the penalties threatening to reduce representation in Congress were never enforced.*

Section 3. No person shall be a senator or representative in Congress, or elector of President or vice president, or hold any office, civil or military, under the United States, or under any state, who, having previously taken an oath, as a member of Congress, or as an officer of the United States, or as a member of any state legislature, or as an executive or judicial officer of any state, to support the Constitution of the United States, shall have engaged in insurrection or rebellion against the same, or given aid or comfort to the enemies thereof. But Congress may by a vote of two-thirds of each house, remove such disability.

Anyone who was a member of Congress, or an elector, or who held a civil or military office in one of the states that seceded from the United States during the Civil War shall not be allowed to hold public office. *This section was designed to punish the leaders of the Confederacy. It was removed in 1896 by Congress.*

Section 4. The validity of the public debt of the United States, authorized by law, including debts incurred for payment of pensions and bounties for services in suppressing insurrection or rebellion, shall not be questioned. But neither the United States nor any state shall assume or pay any debt or obligation incurred in aid of insurrection or rebellion against the United States, or any claim for the loss of emancipation of any slave; but all such debts, obligations and claims shall be held illegal and void.

Section 5. The Congress shall have power to enforce, by appropriate legislation, the provisions of this article.

Amendment XV

Section 1. The right of citizens of the United States to vote shall not be denied or abridged by the United States or by any state on account of race, color, or previous condition of servitude.

Section 2. The Congress shall have power to enforce this article by appropriate legislation.

All debts and pensions and payments of the Union shall be honored and paid without question. All debts and pensions and payments accrued by those states in rebellion (the Confederacy) cannot and will not be paid by the federal government. Nor can any payments be made for those slaves.

Congress has the power to make laws that will enforce the statements made in this amendment.

African Americans Given the Right to Vote

The right of citizens of the United States to vote shall not be denied by the United States nor by any state because of race, color, or because of past service as a slave.

Congress has the power to make laws that will enforce the statements made in this amendment.

120

The End of Slavery

Amendments XIII, XIV, and XV

1. Lincoln's Emancipation Proclamation freed the slaves. So, why was the 13th Amendment necessary?

    _____

2. What citizenship rights were granted or protected by Section 1 of the 14th Amendment?

    _____

    _____

3. What was the original intention of the 14th Amendment, Section 1?

    _____

4. How does the 14th Amendment, Section 2, change the census from the way it was taken according to Article 1, Section 2?

    _____

    _____

5. What qualifications for voting were set by the 14th Amendment, Section 2?

    _____

6. What was the penalty imposed on a state that denied qualified voters their legal right to vote?

    _____

    _____

7. According to the 14th Amendment, no person shall hold a government office who once took an oath of office swearing to uphold the Constitution, and then engaged himself in a rebellion against the United States. This section took away many good leaders from the South and created a situation of corrupt government when certain "carpetbaggers" from the North rushed to the South to claim the political positions made available by the rule. Such restrictions could only be removed by a _____ vote of the members of Congress. This was finally done in 1896.

8. Review Section 4 of the 14th Amendment. What was the major difference in the payment of the war debts of the South and payment of the war debts of the North?

_____

_____

_____

9. The 14th Amendment outlined citizenship and the requirements for representation (which included African Americans). Why do you suppose Congress wrote the 15th Amendment?

_____

_____

_____

10. Why do you think the 15th Amendment did not specify the right to vote for African Americans?

_____

_____

_____

11. Research and describe the methods some Southern states used to avoid following the 14th Amendment.

_____

_____

_____

_____

_____

Amendment XVI

Income Tax

The Congress shall have power to lay and collect taxes on incomes, from whatever source derived, without apportionment among the several states, and without regard to any census or enumeration.

Congress shall have the power to assess a tax on all individual incomes, regardless of the sources from which they come. The amount of money collected will not be divided equally among the states nor the people. *Prior to the 16th Amendment, the federal government relied mostly on tariffs and excise taxes to support its functions financially. Taxes assessed on individual incomes would provide the government much more money. Those who supported the amendment believed that everyone should pay to support the government according to his or her ability to pay.*

1. Why are income taxes collected? What are these funds used for? List the programs, amenities, and services that we enjoy which might be at least partially funded by income taxes.

_____

_____

_____

_____

2. What is your opinion of income tax? Is it fair to ask everyone to pay the same amount? Why or why not?

_____

_____

_____

_____

Amendment XVII

Direct Election of Senators

The Senate of the United States shall be composed of two senators from each state, elected by the people thereof for six years; and each senator shall have one vote. The electors in each state shall have the qualifications requisite for electors of the most numerous branch of the state legislatures.

When vacancies happen in the representation of any state in the Senate, the executive authority of such state shall issue writs of election to fill such vacancies: *Provided*, That the legislature of any state may empower the executive thereof to make temporary appointments until the people fill the vacancies by election as the legislature may direct.

This amendment shall not be so construed as to affect the election or term of any senator chosen before it becomes valid as part of the Constitution.

The Senate shall consist of two senators from each state, elected by the people for six-year terms. Each senator shall have one vote. People who are qualified to vote in the elections for the largest house in their own state legislature may also vote in the elections for the two U.S. senators who serve their state.

Whenever a vacancy shall occur in the Senate, the governor of the state affected shall call for a special election to fill that vacancy. However, the governor may be empowered by the state legislature to appoint a temporary replacement until the general election is held.

This amendment shall not affect the election or term of office for anyone serving in the Senate at the time it becomes a part of the Constitution.

1. How did the 17th Amendment change the way U.S. senators were to be elected?

_____

_____

_____

2. What are the two alternatives to filling a vacancy in the U.S. Senate?

_____

_____

_____

Amendment XVIII

Prohibition

Section 1. After one year from the ratification of this article the manufacture, sale, or transportation of intoxicating liquors within, the importation thereof into, or the exportation thereof from the United States and all territory subject to the jurisdiction thereof for beverage purposes is hereby prohibited.

One year after ratification of this amendment, it shall be illegal to manufacture, sell, or transport alcoholic liquors anywhere in the United States and its territories. It shall be illegal to export alcoholic liquors out of the country or to import them into the United States or its territories.

Section 2. The Congress and the several states shall have concurrent power to enforce this article by appropriate legislation.

The Congress and the state legislatures shall share in the power to enforce this amendment through appropriate legislation. *The Volstead Act passed by Congress provided most of the specific law needed to put teeth into the amendment and define the penalties for violating the law.*

Section 3. This article shall be inoperative unless it shall have been ratified as an amendment to the Constitution by the legislatures of the several states, as provided in the Constitution, within seven years from the date of the submission hereof to the states by the Congress.

This amendment shall not become effective unless it is ratified by three-fourths of the state legislatures within seven years from the date of its submission to the state by Congress. *Beginning with this amendment, it became common practice to allow a period of seven years between proposal and ratification. If a proposed amendment did not receive proper ratification within that time period, then it would be dropped.*

1. When was the 18th Amendment ratified?

_____

2. Research the Volstead Act and explain how it is connected to the 18th Amendment.

_____

_____

Progressive Era

Imagine you are a member of a reform group during the Progressive Era. Research one of the major issues of that time, such as labor practices, votes for women, government reform, or the prohibition of alcohol. Write a column for a pamphlet about this issue explaining what you think should be done to correct the problem. Try to convince your readers to agree with your opinion. Connect your opinion to one of the constitutional amendments.

_____

_____

_____

_____

_____

_____

_____

_____

_____

_____

_____

_____

_____

_____

_____

_____

_____

Amendment XIX

Section 1. The right of citizens of the United States to vote shall not be denied or abridged by the United States or by any state on account of sex.

Section 2. Congress shall have power to enforce this article by appropriate legislation.

Woman Suffrage

The right of citizens of the United States to vote cannot be denied by the United States nor by any state because of sex.

Congress has the power to make laws that will enforce this amendment. *Suffrage is defined as the privilege of voting.*

076822456X • Our Living Constitution

Woman Suffrage

Amendment XIX

Women earned the right to vote in 1920 when the 19th Amendment was ratified as part of the United States Constitution. Although Susan B. Anthony did not live to see her dream fulfilled, she is considered one of the early champions of women's rights.

Research Susan B. Anthony and write a brief biographical sketch of this determined woman. Include details of her life and an explanation of the causes to which she dedicated her life.

_____

_____

_____

_____

_____

_____

_____

_____

_____

_____

_____

_____

_____

_____

_____

_____

Amendment XX

Lame Duck Amendment

Under the original Constitution, the newly elected President took office on March 4 following the November election. Newly elected members of Congress waited until the following December before the next session began. Between the time of election and the time when the new President and members of Congress took office, the old President and members of Congress continued in office. This time period was called a "lame duck" time. Those who had either been voted out of office or chose not to run for reelection were virtually powerless, and the country lacked solid leadership during this period. The main purpose of the 20th Amendment was to shorten the period between election day and the time when the newly elected President and members of Congress took office.

Section 1. The terms of the President and vice president shall end at noon on the twentieth day of January, and the terms of senators and representatives at noon on the third day of January, of the year in which such terms would have ended if this article had not been ratified; and the terms of their successors shall then begin.

The terms of office for the President and the vice president shall end at noon on January 20; and the terms of office for senators and representatives shall end at noon on January 3. These terms end in the same year they would have ended if this amendment had not been ratified, and the terms of their successors shall begin at that time.

Section 2. The Congress shall assemble at least once in every year, and such meeting shall begin at noon on the third day of January, unless they shall by law appoint a different day.

Congress shall meet at least once every year, beginning at noon on January 3, unless Congress chooses a different day to begin its meetings. *This session begins on January 3, but continues open all year with the exception of weekends and occasional recesses as chosen by Congress. It may also choose to adjust its opening if January 3 should fall on a weekend.*

Section 3. If, at the time fixed for the beginning of the term of the President, the President elect shall have died, the vice president elect shall become President. If a President shall not have been chosen before the time fixed for the beginning of his term, or if the President elect shall have failed to qualify, then the vice president elect shall act as President until a President shall have qualified; and the Congress may by law provide for the case wherein neither a President elect nor a vice president elect shall have qualified, declaring who shall then act as President, or the manner in which one who is to act shall be selected, and such person shall act accordingly until a President or vice president shall have qualified.

Section 4. The Congress may by law provide for the case of the death of any of the persons from whom the House of Representatives may choose a President whenever the right of choice shall have devolved upon them, and for the case of the death of any of the persons from whom the Senate may choose a vice president whenever the right of choice shall have devolved upon them.

Section 5. Sections 1 and 2 shall take effect on the 15th day of October following the ratification of this article.

Section 6. This article shall be inoperative unless it shall have been ratified as an amendment to the Constitution by the legislatures of three-fourths of the several states within seven years from the date of its submission.

If the President-elect should die before actually assuming the office, then the vice president-elect shall become President. If a President has not been chosen by January 20, or if the person chosen should fail to qualify, then the vice president-elect shall fill in as the President until one is chosen. Congress can pass a law to decide who shall act as President if no one has been officially elected as President or as vice president. The person so designated shall serve only until a President or vice president is properly elected.

Congress shall have the power to make a law to determine what to do in the case of the House of Representatives having to elect the President and that chosen person dying before he assumes office. Congress also has the power to decide what shall be done in the event that the Senate must choose a vice president and that person dies before assuming office.

Sections 1 and 2 shall take effect on the fifteenth of October that follows proper ratification of this amendment.

This amendment shall be dropped if it has not been ratified by three-fourths of the state legislatures within seven years of its formal proposal.

076822456X • Our Living Constitution

Name_____

Lame Duck Amendment

Amendment XX

1. How often is Congress required to meet and on what day does the session begin?

   _____

2. How is the lame duck period shortened by the 20th Amendment? Include information for the President and vice president and Congress.

   _____

   _____

   _____

3. What will happen if the House of Representatives is forced to elect the President and their choice should die before assuming office?

   _____

   _____

4. Why do you think the term *lame duck* is used to define the period between the time of election and assumption of office?

   _____

   _____

   _____

5. When do the terms of office begin for the new President and vice president?

   _____

6. When does the term begin for the newly elected members of Congress?

   _____

7. Research the 2000 presidential election. According to the 20th Amendment, what might have happened if a President had not been officially elected by January 20?

The 18th Amendment prohibited the manufacture, sale, or transportation of alcohol. The strength and organization of the progressive reformers was effective for getting the 18th Amendment ratified. Yet, the restrictions were much more difficult to enforce. There were not enough agents to enforce the Volstead Act. Americans had just survived the "war-to-end-all-wars" (World War I) and there was a feeling of optimism in the air. It became a time of carefree living and good times.

Since the taverns and nightclubs were closed, some people gathered in illegal clubs called *speakeasies*. People could get liquor made illegally here in the United States or smuggled in from abroad. This *bootlegging* and illegal traffic in liquor was highly profitable to those who dared to participate, and the competition over this illegal trade soon spawned a great deal of crime and violence. The "noble experiment" had failed. To bring an end to the failure, the 18th Amendment was repealed by the 21st Amendment.

Amendment XXI

Section 1. The eighteenth article of amendment to the Constitution of the United States is hereby repealed.

Section 2. The transportation or importation into any state, territory, or possession of the United States for delivery or use therein of intoxicating liquors, in violation of the laws thereof, is hereby prohibited.

Section 3. This article shall be inoperative unless it shall have been ratified as an amendment to the Constitution by conventions in the several states, as provided in the Constitution, within seven years from the date of the submission hereof to the states by the Congress.

The Repeal of Prohibition

The 18th Amendment to the Constitution is hereby repealed. Prohibition is no longer a part of federal laws.

The transporting or importing of alcohol into any state which prohibits liquor is against federal laws, too. *Even though Prohibition was outlawed at the national level, the amendment still recognized the rights of individual states to remain "dry."*

This amendment shall be inoperative if it is not ratified by special conventions in three-fourths of the states within seven years of the date of its formal proposal. *Congress decided to place this amendment before special state conventions for ratification rather than allow the state legislatures to decide. In less than eight months, conventions had ratified the amendment in enough states to make it law.*

Repeal of Prohibition

Amendment XXI

1. What caused the 18th Amendment to be repealed?

_____

_____

_____

2. Although Article 5 of the Constitution provides for two methods in ratifying amendments, the 21st Amendment is the only one to be ratified by special conventions held in the various states. All of the other twenty-five were ratified by the state legislatures. Why did Congress decide to have this one ratified through special convention?

_____

_____

_____

3. Even though alcohol was made legal again by the 21st Amendment, the Prohibitionist movement never completely died. The Prohibitionist party remains the third oldest political party in the United States. Although it never wins any offices, its candidates always earn a few votes in each presidential election. Find out what the Prohibitionist party stands for besides banning the sale and use of alcohol.

_____

_____

_____

The 22nd Amendment was prompted by Americans who questioned the length of time a President should serve. Prior to 1940, presidents had served only one or two terms of office. But in 1940, Franklin D. Roosevelt was elected a third time and in 1944 ran again and won. Many Americans felt this was too long for one man to serve. The result was the 22nd Amendment.

Amendment XXII

Section 1. No person shall be elected to the office of the President more than twice, and no person who has held the office of President, or acted as President, for more than two years of a term to which some other person was elected President shall be elected to the office of the President more than once. But this article shall not apply to any person holding the office of President when this article was proposed by the Congress, and shall not prevent any person who may be holding the office of President, or acting as President, during the term within which this article becomes operative from holding the office of President or acting as President during the remainder of such term.

President's Term of Office

No person can be elected to the office of the President more than twice, and anyone who has served in the capacity of President for more than two years of someone else's term can only be elected once. But this article does not apply to the person holding office at the time of its proposal (Harry Truman), nor will it affect the President in office or person holding the office at the time of its ratification. *Ten years is the maximum amount of time any single individual can serve as President. Conceivably someone who served as vice president could become President (if the office were to be vacated) and serve out the two years or less remaining on that term of office, then be elected President twice in his own right. But if the unexpired term he fulfilled was longer than two years, then he could be elected only once.*

Section 2. This article shall be inoperative unless it shall have been ratified as an amendment to the Constitution by the legislatures of three-fourths of the several states within seven years from the date of its submission to the states by the Congress.

This amendment will be dropped if it is not properly ratified within seven years of the time of its formal proposal.

Presidential Term Limit

Amendment XXII

1. Which President prompted the adoption of the 22nd Amendment? Why was it added as a change in the Constitution?

    _____

    _____

2. Who was the first President to be affected by the rules as described in the 22nd Amendment?

    _____

3. If the term of office for a U.S. President is four years and a President can only serve two terms in office, explain how someone could conceivably serve as President for ten years.

    _____

    _____

4. In 1973, Spiro Agnew resigned as vice president. President Richard Nixon appointed Gerald Ford as the new vice president. On August 9, 1974, Nixon resigned from the presidency and Gerald Ford became President. Could Gerald Ford have sought the presidency himself in the election of 1976? Could Ford have run again in 1980 if he had won in 1976?

    _____

    _____

5. There are advantages and disadvantages to having a national leader serve as head of a country for an extended period of time. List some advantages and disadvantages then choose one side of the argument to support. Write a brief essay supporting your position.

    _____

    _____

    _____

    _____

    _____

The District of Columbia

Because the nation's capital, Washington, D.C., was not a part of any state, its citizens were not allowed to vote in presidential and congressional elections. The 23rd Amendment provided them with a method to vote for the President and vice president, but Washington, D.C. still does not have true representation in Congress. The city is allowed one nonvoting member to sit in the House of Representatives, but he or she can only voice an opinion.

Amendment XXIII

Section 1. The district constituting the seat of government of the United States shall appoint in such manner as the Congress may direct:

A number of electors of President and vice president equal to the whole number of senators and representatives in Congress to which the District would be entitled if it were a state, but in no event more than the least populous state; they shall be in addition to those appointed by the states, but they shall be considered, for the purposes of the election of President and vice president, to be electors appointed by a state; and they shall meet in the district and perform such duties as provided by the twelfth article of amendment.

Section 2. The Congress shall have power to enforce this article by appropriate legislation.

Electoral Votes for Washington, D.C.

The District of Columbia (Washington, D.C.) shall be allowed the same number of electors as it would have if it were a state, but that number cannot exceed the least populous state. The electors chosen to represent the District of Columbia shall follow the same rules and perform the same duties as the electors of the states as set forth in the 12th Amendment. *Although Washington, D.C., has a population more than twice that of the entire state of Alaska, the amendment restricts the city to three electors.*

Congress shall have the power to make laws to enforce the amendment.

1. Washington, D.C., has three electoral votes. Why is it limited to three?

_____

_____

2. With the 23rd Amendment, how many total electors are in the Electoral College?

_____

3. How many electors does it take to win the presidency?

_____

Amendment XXIV

Poll Tax Abolished

Section 1. The right of citizens of the United States to vote in any primary or other election for President or vice president, for electors for President or vice president, or for senator or representative in Congress, shall not be denied or abridged by the United States or any state by reason of failure to pay any poll tax or other tax.

The right of citizens to vote in primary or other elections for President, vice president, senators, or representatives shall not be denied by the United States nor by any state because of a failure to pay a poll tax. Some states discriminated against people by requiring voters to pay a tax to vote—called a poll tax. This amendment outlawed such taxes for national elections. States were allowed to assess poll taxes on state elections, but this was difficult because national officials often would be elected in the same election.

Section 2. The Congress shall have the power to enforce this article by appropriate legislation.

Congress shall have the power to make laws to enforce this amendment.

1. What was a poll tax?

   _____

   _____

2. Why did some states charge a poll tax?

   _____

   _____

3. Although the 24th Amendment did not eliminate poll taxes for state elections, how did it discourage them?

   _____

   _____

Section 1.
In case of the removal of the President from office or his death or resignation, the vice president shall become President.

Section 2.
Whenever there is a vacancy in the office of the vice president, the President shall nominate a vice president who shall take office upon confirmation by a majority vote of both houses of Congress.

Section 3.
Whenever the President transmits to the president pro tempore of the Senate and the Speaker of the House of Representatives his written declaration that he is unable to discharge the powers and duties of his office, and until he transmits to them a written declaration to the contrary, such powers and duties shall be discharged by the vice president as acting President.

Section 4.
Whenever the vice president and a majority of either the principal officers of the executive departments or of such other body as Congress may by law provide, transmit to the president pro tempore of the Senate and the Speaker of the House of Representatives their written declaration that the President is unable to discharge the powers and duties of his office, the vice president shall immediately assume the powers and duties of the office as acting President.

Amendment XXV – Presidential Disability and Succession

The original Constitution provided no plan to replace the vice president when he or she moved up to fill a vacancy in the presidency. The 25th Amendment corrected this problem. It also provided for a smooth transition for times when the vice president needs to take over for the President temporarily.

If the President is removed from office, dies, or resigns, the vice president becomes the President.

When a vacancy occurs in the office of vice president, the President shall appoint someone who will take the office upon approval by a majority of both houses of Congress.

When the President notifies in writing the president pro tempore of the Senate and the Speaker of the House of Representatives that he is unable to perform his duties as President, then the vice president shall serve as acting President.

When the vice president and a majority of the members of the cabinet feel the President is unable to perform the duties of his office, they shall notify the president pro tempore of the Senate and the Speaker of the House of Representatives. Upon such notification, the vice president immediately becomes the acting President.

Thereafter, when the President transmits to the president pro tempore of the Senate and the Speaker of the House of Representatives his written declaration that no inability exists, he shall resume the powers and duties of his office unless the vice president and a majority of either the principal officers of the executive department or of such other body as Congress may by law provide, transmit within four days to the president pro tempore of the Senate and the Speaker of the House of Representatives their written declaration that the President is unable to discharge the powers and duties of his office. Thereupon Congress shall decide the issue, assembling within forty-eight hours for that purpose if not in session. If the Congress, within twenty-one days after receipt of the latter written declaration, or, if Congress is not in session, within twenty-one days after Congress is required to assemble, determines by two-thirds vote of both houses that the President is unable to discharge the powers and duties of his office, the vice president shall continue to discharge the same as acting President; otherwise, the President shall resume the powers and duties of his office.

When the President feels he has recovered from his disability or illness, he shall submit a written acknowledgment of such to the president pro tempore of the Senate and the Speaker of the House of Representatives. If the vice president feels the President has not completely recovered, he or she and a majority of the cabinet must notify the leaders of the two houses of Congress within four days. Congress shall have 48 hours to assemble if its members are not in session and have 21 days to discuss the issues. If two-thirds of both houses agree that the President is still unable to fulfill his duties, then the vice president shall continue acting as President.

Presidential Disability

1. When Lyndon Johnson became President after the assassination of John F. Kennedy in 1963, there was no one to succeed him as vice president. To correct this problem, the 25th Amendment was proposed in 1965 and ratified in 1967. Research and explain the circumstances in 1973 that led to the first application of the 25th Amendment.

_____

_____

_____

2. Under the terms described in the 25th Amendment, what would prevent an ambitious vice president from claiming the President was ill just so he or she could assume the office as acting President?

_____

_____

_____

3. What does the President have to do when he decides he is ready to resume his duties?

_____

_____

_____

4. The 25th Amendment contains several built-in measures to prevent a President who is seriously ill from serving in our highest office. Who would be the best judge of whether or not a President is able to fulfill his duties as President?

_____

_____

_____

Amendment XXVI

Voting Age

Section 1. The right of citizens of the United States, who are eighteen years of age or older, to vote shall not be denied or abridged by the United States or by any state on account of age.

Section 2. The Congress shall have power to enforce this article by appropriate legislation.

The right of citizens to vote who are eighteen years of age or older shall not be denied by the United States nor by any state because of age.

Congress shall have the power to enforce this amendment through appropriate legislation.

1. The 26th Amendment granted the right to vote for all citizens over 18 years of age. Research the voting procedures in your state. What do citizens need to do in order to register to vote? What are the other requirements for voting privileges?

_____

_____

_____

_____

2. Many people feel the voting age should be a minimum of 21 years. What do you think? Are 18-year-olds responsible enough to vote? What about 15-year-olds or 13-year-olds? What should be the standards for voting? Provide evidence to support your argument.

_____

_____

_____

_____

Amendment XXVII

Pay Raises for Members of Congress

No law varying the compensation for the services of the senators and representatives shall take effect, until an election of representatives shall have intervened.

Any pay raises voted by members of Congress can only become effective following the next election of U.S. representatives.

1. The 27th Amendment to the Constitution became a reality in 1992. Why was the amendment added to the Constitution?

_____

_____

_____

2. Who do you think was the driving influence behind this Constitutional change?

_____

_____

3. What was the logic behind allowing pay raises to follow the next election of U.S. representatives (elected every two years) rather than the election of U.S. senators (every six years)?

_____

_____

_____

4. What is the current salary of U.S. representatives? What is the current salary of U.S. senators?

_____

_____

Our Amendments at Work

Below are examples of constitutional amendments at work. Read each statement and decide which constitutional amendment is at work. Place the number of the correct amendment in the blank space provided.

1. _____ Olivia Philips is a county sheriff. She goes to the home of Raymond Johnson and demands entry into his house. Even though he has nothing to hide, Johnson tells Philips to "Buzz off! You don't even have a search warrant." Which constitutional amendment allows Johnson this protection?

2. _____ The Longhurst family has the right to plan their family vacation to any place they want to go. They wouldn't necessarily have this right in some other countries of the world. Which amendment gives the Longhurst family this right?

3. _____ Any African American or member of any other minority who qualifies can vote in the United States because of this amendment. Which one is it?

4. _____ If either of the two U.S. senators from the state of Ohio should become incapable of performing his or her duties, then it would be up to the governor of Ohio to find someone to fill the vacant office, or to call for a special election. In which amendment is this provision found?

5. _____ Mary Anne Wilcox voted for Franklin D. Roosevelt in the general election of 1932. Which amendment enabled her to do so?

6. _____ If Officer Garcia arrests Mr. O'Conner for speeding and O'Conner claims he is innocent, it then becomes Garcia's word against O'Conner's (since Garcia did not have a radar gun). O'Conner really believes he is innocent, but he figures the judge will probably believe Garcia because he is a law officer. The penalty will be O'Conner's third within a year; and, as a result, he will lose his license for six months if he is found guilty. He does believe, however, that the judgment of twelve good people will decide in his favor; therefore, he demands a jury trial. Where in the Constitution is O'Conner guaranteed this right?

7. _____ The local newspaper prints an editorial column criticizing the mayor's spending of public funds. Which amendment protects this right?

8. _____ The Donovans and the Patels are at odds over the location of the boundary line dividing their properties. The area in question dates back to a mistake made when the land was originally surveyed and amounts to just under one-half acre altogether. Since the two families cannot agree on a settlement, they have decided to put the matter before a jury in a court of law. This they can do because of which constitutional amendment?

9. _____ In the election of 1800, it became clear that the framers of the Constitution made a mistake in having the person with the second highest number of votes become vice president. That was all changed in 1804 by what amendment?

10. _____ This amendment had the effect of canceling the "three-fifths clause" (Article 1, Section 7, clause 3), which counted only three-fifths of the slaves for purposes of determining representation in Congress and taxation.

11. _____ Nate Williams lives in the state of Louisiana. Years ago, Nate's father was not allowed to vote in state and local elections because he could not pay the poll tax. He couldn't afford to buy his right to vote because he considered food and shelter more important. Nate, however, can vote in national elections because of an amendment in the Constitution that forbids the use of a poll tax in national elections. Which one?

12. _____ George W. Bush became the nation's 43rd President on Saturday, January 20, 2001, at 12:00 noon EST. He was sworn into office by Chief Justice William Rehnquist. Under the original Constitution, Mr. Bush would have had to wait until March 4 to take over as President. Which constitutional amendment changed the inauguration dates?

13. _____ Jeffrey Gallagher was suspected and finally arrested for the murder of Sergio Navarro. There were no eyewitnesses to the shooting. Gallagher had a motive, but he also had a fairly legitimate alibi that explained his whereabouts at the time of the shooting. He told his friend, Jan Bonovich, "I am not really worried. There isn't enough evidence to even bring me to trial." He was right. The Grand Jury failed to find enough evidence against Gallagher to even bring him to trial, and he was released under a "no true bill" statement. This right given to Gallagher is ensured to all of us because of which constitutional amendment?

14. _____ Kay Fujimoto keeps a gun in her closet. Kay tells all of her friends that she keeps it there to defend herself against anyone who would try to break into her home. Kay could get herself into a whole lot of trouble if she uses that gun without caution, but Kay's right to keep the weapon to defend herself is protected by which constitutional amendment?

15. _____ The U.S. Army's budget has been drastically reduced and army officials are scrambling to find adequate housing for the soldiers. The army has decided to place one soldier in each home in America to solve the problem. Which amendment prevents this from happening during a time of peace?

16. _____ U.S. Congresswoman Janelle Brown recently voted in favor of raising the pay of members of Congress. Before Brown can cash in on her pay raise, she must first face re-election back in her home state. This change in the Constitution became a reality in which constitutional amendment?

17. _____ Each week the federal government takes out a percentage of Earl Thompson's paycheck. The power to levy an income tax in order to pay for the services of the federal government is granted in which amendment?

18. _____ Tiffany Dobson is 19 years old. She will be voting for the first time in the upcoming presidential election. Which amendment lowered the voting age to 18 years of age?

19. _____ The citizens of Washington, D.C., are allowed to vote for President, too. This right had been denied before because only states were given electors, and Washington, D.C., is not a state. Which amendment changed all this to allow the citizens of the nation's capital the right to vote in presidential elections?

20. _____ Arnold Gross, formerly of Athens, Georgia, now living in Jackson, Mississippi, lodges a protest against the state of Georgia. He feels his business was unfairly taxed when he lived in Georgia. He even attempts to file a formal lawsuit against the state of Georgia; however, there is no place for the case to be heard. The federal courts will not hear cases involving citizens of one state against another state. This is clearly pointed out in which of the constitutional amendments?

21. _____ Former President Clinton served from 1993 to 2001. Which of the constitutional amendments forbids Clinton from being elected to more than two terms of office?

22. _____ In 1920, Shannon O'Toole converted his tavern into a family restaurant. Because of the prohibition of alcohol, he could no longer serve alcoholic beverages in his tavern. Which amendment prohibited the sale of alcoholic beverages?

23. _____ It is now legal to consume alcoholic beverages as long as the person doing the drinking has satisfied the minimum age requirements. This amendment repealed an earlier amendment and reinstated the legalized consumption of alcohol.

24. _____ In 1974, President Richard Nixon resigned and Vice President Gerald Ford became the President, leaving a vacancy in the vice presidency. Which amendment makes sure there will always be a vice president?

25. _____ Sam Jones is arrested for knocking down Mrs. Wong and stealing her purse, which contained $4.10. At the police station, Sam is treated rather harshly by the officer in charge and is bodily thrown into a cell. He overhears the arresting officer say that they are going to "throw the book" at him for doing such a lowly thing to such a nice little old lady. Sam knows that his penalty cannot be too harsh for committing such a minor offense. Which amendment makes Sam so certain?

26. _____ Which constitutional amendment makes slavery illegal?

27. _____ All powers not delegated to the federal government are reserved for either the states or the people. Which constitutional amendment guarantees this power?

Reviewing the Constitution

Below are some statements about the Constitution which are not true. Read each statement and locate the article, section, and clause in the Constitution that pertains to that statement. Then rewrite each statement to make it true.

1. Congress has no right to meddle in the private affairs of the several states by controlling trade. Location: _____

    _____

    _____

2. Members of the House of Representatives are chosen by the voters every four years. Location:_____

    _____

    _____

3. Congress must have approval from the President on all resolutions to make them take effect. Location: _____

    _____

    _____

4. It is not always necessary to have witnesses who speak against the accused in court. Location: _____

    _____

    _____

5. The term of office for a federal judge is ten years. Location:_____

    _____

    _____

6. All foreign ambassadors nominated by the President need approval by two-thirds of the Senate. Location:_____

    _____

    _____

7. If a majority of the Senate feels a President is unable to resume his office, they must notify his cabinet. Location:_____

_____

_____

8. The President of the United States must be at least thirty years of age. Location:_____

_____

_____

9. If no candidate for President has a majority of the electors, the President is Location:_____

_____

_____

10. A fleeing criminal can escape justice by crossing into another state where he cannot be prosecuted. Location: _____

_____

_____

11. Congress has command over the nation's armed forces. Location:_____

_____

_____

12. Only authorized law enforcement officers have the right to own guns. Location:_____

_____

_____

13. The power of impeachment rests with a majority of both houses of Congress. Location:_____

_____

_____

14. No President can serve more than two terms or eight years. Location:_____

_____

_____

15. Exorbitant fines and punishments can be levied only after an offender's second offense. Location:_____

_____

_____

16. No person shall be convicted of treason without the testimony of an eyewitness. Location:_____

_____

_____

17. New states can only be admitted to the Union by approval of the President and a vote of two-thirds of Congress. Location: _____

_____

_____

18. To amend the Constitution requires ratification by two-thirds of the state legislatures. Location: _____

_____

_____

19. The government cannot buy the land of those who do not wish to sell. Location: _____

_____

_____

20. Individual states can coin their own money only with the approval of Congress. Location: _____

_____

_____

We the People

Challenge your students to share their knowledge of the Constitution with this exciting game. The 160 trivia questions are based on the contents of the Constitution and related topics students have learned in their study of the Constitution. There are four questions on the front of each of the 40 cards. The answers can be found on the backs of the cards. To make the cards more durable, reproduce them on cardstock and laminate them before cutting apart.

Directions for Play

1. Divide the class into teams of three to five students.

2. Give each team a die. Determine which team will play first by having a representative from each team roll the die. The team with the highest number will play first.

3. The teacher acts as the game host and shuffles the cards.

4. The first team to play rolls their die. The number on the die indicates which question the host reads to the team. For example, if the team rolls a three, the host reads question number three on the card. If a five is rolled, the team answers the question of their choice and gets double points for answering correctly. If the team rolls a six, they lose a turn.

5. The team has ten seconds to confer about the answer. Then a representative for the team reports the answer. The first answer given is the final answer. If the answer is correct, the team earns one point (unless a five had been rolled).

6. If the answer is incorrect, the next team gets the same question.

7. The first team to reach twenty points wins the game.

Variations

Adjust the rules to follow a similar format to popular game shows.

Two players can quiz each other.

Reproduce the entire page for test preparation.

Play the game in a spelling-bee format.

Children line up in four lines and give each student one question from a card.

Note: Reproduce pages 150 to 159 as two-sided photocopies. The questions and answers must correspond as given.

1. Our country's first framework of national government

2. The year our present Constitution was written

3. The city where the Constitution was written

4. The building where the Constitution was written

---

1. Unlike Article 3 of the Constitution, the Articles of Confederation made no provisions for these.

2. Because the Articles of Confederation did not provide for a strong central government, this was written.

3. He presided over the Constitutional Convention.

4. He wrote the Constitution in its final form.

---

1. The date the Constitution was signed

2. The number of men who signed the original Constitution

3. The number of states represented at the Convention

4. The only state not represented at the Constitutional Convention

---

1. The number of branches in our federal government

2. The legislative arm of our national government

3. The judicial branch of our federal government

4. The leader of our executive department

---

1. The number of amendments added to the Constitution under the Bill of Rights

2. The name given to the first ten amendments

3. The year the Constitution became the law of the land

4. The body which makes our laws.

---

1. The number of representatives in Congress

2. The number of representatives a state gets is determined by this.

3. The length of term of office for a U.S. representative

4. The title given those who serve in the House of Representatives

---

1. The title given to those who serve in the U.S. Senate

2. The minimum age requirement for members of the House of Representatives

3. The census is taken every _____ years.

4. The title of the leader of the House of Representatives

---

1. The minimum length of time as a U.S. citizen required of a member of the House of Representatives

2. They choose the Speaker of the House.

3. The minimum number of representatives a state may have

4. They have the power of impeachment.

1. courts

2. Constitution

3. George Washington

4. Gouverneur Morris

---

1. Articles of Confederation

2. 1787

3. Philadelphia

4. Independence Hall

---

1. 3

2. Congress

3. U.S. courts

4. President

---

1. Sept. 17, 1787

2. 39

3. 12

4. Rhode Island

---

1. 435

2. population

3. 2 years

4. congressperson

---

1. 10

2. Bill of Rights

3. 1788

4. Congressmen

---

1. 7 years

2. House of Representatives

3. 1

4. House of Representatives

---

1. senators

2. 25

3. 10 years

4. speaker

---

1. The body that tries those who have been impeached

2. The length of term for a U.S. senator

3. The minimum length of time as a U.S. citizen required for a U.S. senator

4. The number of senators in the U.S. Senate

---

1. The number of senators from each state

2. The minimum age requirement for a U.S. senator

3. He or she presides over the U.S. Senate.

4. One-third of the U.S. Senate is elected every _____ years.

---

1. Makes the rules concerning U.S. citizenship

2. Has the power to issue currency

3. Has the power to declare war

4. A formal objection by the President of a bill sent him by Congress

---

1. He or she presides over the trial of an impeached President.

2. The vote required to convict one who has been impeached

3. The official minutes of Congress

4. The vote needed to expel a member of the House or the Senate

---

1. The number of members of the House required in attendance to conduct business

2. The number of members of the Senate required to constitute a quorum

3. The vote required to make public the vote of each member of Congress

4. The number of electors in the Electoral College

---

1. The number of electoral votes needed to win the presidency

2. Congress is required to meet at least how many times per year?

3. The maximum length of time one house may adjourn without consent from the other house

4. The origin of tax bills

---

1. The vote required in Congress to override a presidential veto

2. The time period a President has to act on a bill sent him by Congress

3. A court order requiring that someone being held in jail be shown justifiable reason for being detained

4. A law that would punish a person for doing something that was not against the law when it was done

---

1. The length of the term of office for a President

2. The number of electors each state has

3. They officially elect the President.

4. The maximum number of terms to which a President may be elected

---

1. 2

2. 30

3. Vice President

4. 2

1. Senate

2. 6 years

3. 9 years

4. 100

1. Chief Justice of the Supreme Court

2. 2/3 of the senators present

3. Congressional Record

4. 2/3

1. Congress

2. Congress

3. Congress

4. veto

1. 270

2. once each year

3. 3 days

4. House of Representatives

1. 218

2. 51

3. 1/5

4. 538

1. 4 years

2. its number of senators plus representatives

3. Electoral College

4. two

1. 2/3

2. 10 days

3. writ of habeas corpus

4. ex post facto law

Card 1

1. He was the only President elected four times.

2. The longest a President can now possibly serve

3. The age requirement for a U.S. President

4. The minimum number of years a U.S. President must live in the United States

Card 2

1. Inauguration Day for the President and the Vice President

2. He or she presides over the Senate in the absence of the Vice President.

3. He or she shall take over for the president in the event the President cannot serve.

4. This office follows the vice president in the line of succession to the President.

Card 3

1. Possesses the power to make treaties with foreign nations

2. The necessary approval to validate all foreign treaties

3. Has the power to nominate federal judges

4. The number of judges on the Supreme Court

Card 4

1. The length of term of office for a U.S. judge

2. The date when Congress begins

3. The highest court in the judicial system

4. Has the power to admit states into the Union

Card 5

1. The number of witnesses necessary to convict someone of treason

2. The court order allowing an authorized search of a person's home and property

3. Trial by jury is guaranteed to all by the _____ Amendment.

4. To become a part of the Constitution, an amendment must be ratified by what fraction of the state legislatures?

Card 6

1. To propose a constitutional amendment requires what fraction of both houses of Congress?

2. An amendment may become a part of the Constitution if it gets approval by special conventions in what fraction of the states?

3. An amendment may be formally proposed by a special convention called by what fraction of the states?

4. The amendment to the Constitution that allows the federal government to tax incomes

Card 7

1. The time between the election of new officials and the time they take office

2. The title of the head judge on the Supreme Court

3. The name given to the judges on the Supreme Court

4. The length of time that most amendments now have to be ratified

Card 8

1. The number of articles in the original Constitution

2. The number of amendments to the Constitution

3. Has the authority to recognize the government of a new nation

4. That part of the Constitution that allows a person the right not to testify against himself

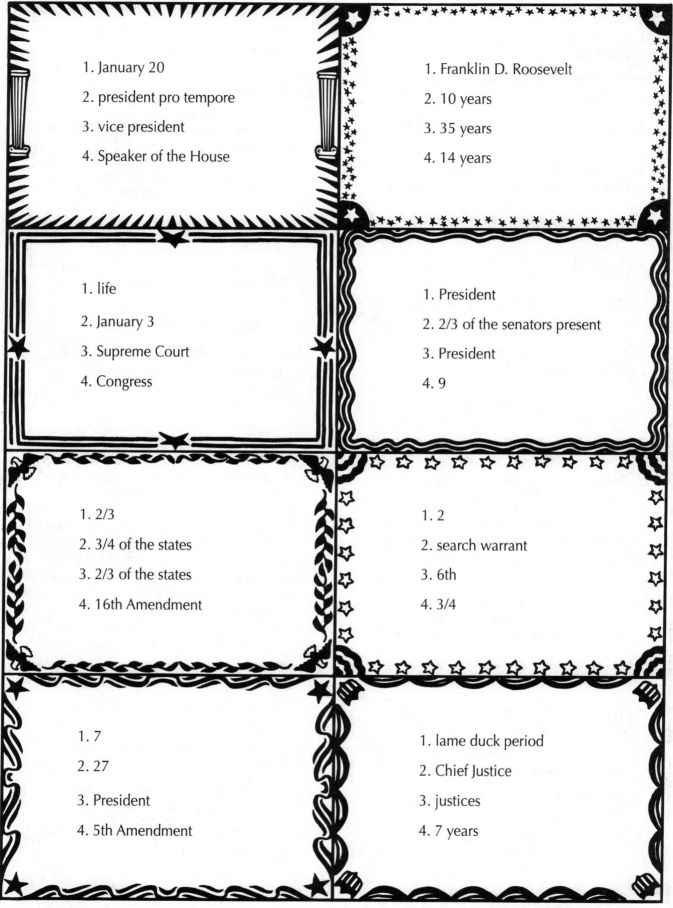

1. January 20
2. president pro tempore
3. vice president
4. Speaker of the House

1. Franklin D. Roosevelt
2. 10 years
3. 35 years
4. 14 years

1. life
2. January 3
3. Supreme Court
4. Congress

1. President
2. 2/3 of the senators present
3. President
4. 9

1. 2/3
2. 3/4 of the states
3. 2/3 of the states
4. 16th Amendment

1. 2
2. search warrant
3. 6th
4. 3/4

1. 7
2. 27
3. President
4. 5th Amendment

1. lame duck period
2. Chief Justice
3. justices
4. 7 years

076822456X • Our Living Constitution

1. The amendment that guarantees the voting rights of women

2. If no candidate for President wins a majority of the electors, who chooses the President?

3. If no candidate for vice president wins a majority of the electors, who chooses the vice president?

4. A system of government which separates the powers between the states and the central government is called a _____.

---

1. The President's group of chief advisors

2. How many positions are there in the President's cabinet?

3. The amendment which was later repealed

4. A court order requiring the appearance of a witness named by the defendant

---

1. The path to U.S. citizenship other than by birth

2. The system which has built-in safeguards against excessive power to any one branch of government

3. A proposed law

4. A formal written accusation issued by a grand jury

---

1. A less serious crime punishable by a short jail sentence or fine

2. Aiding the enemy or selling the secrets of the United States

3. The number of persons on a petit jury

4. The vote needed by a petit jury to reach a decision

---

1. The vote needed by the Supreme Court to reach a decision

2. The amendment that allows us to bear arms to defend ourselves

3. Being tried twice for the same crime

4. The right of the government to take land from a private individual for the good of all

---

1. The jury that determines the guilt or innocence of the accused

2. The constitutional amendment that guarantees free speech

3. The article that contains the full faith and credit clause

4. The constitutional amendment that freed the slaves

---

1. The amendment that outlawed the poll tax in national elections

2. An opening statement of purpose

3. The right to vote

4. Those powers specifically given Congress in Article 1, Section 8

---

1. The term used to define the indirect power of Congress as described in the last paragraph of Article 1, Section 8

2. If the President fails to act on a bill within ten days before Congress adjourns, this is called a _____

3. The length of time the president has to act on a bill passed by Congress

4. Standard procedures followed in a court of law

---

1. the cabinet

2. 14

3. 18th Amendment

4. subpoena

---

1. 19th

2. House of Representatives

3. Senate

4. federal system

---

1. misdemeanor

2. treason

3. 12

4. unanimous, 12-0

---

1. naturalization

2. checks and balances

3. bill

4. indictment

---

1. petit jury

2. 1st Amendment

3. Article 4

4. 13th

---

1. simple majority, 5-4

2. 2nd

3. double jeopardy

4. eminent domain

---

1. implied powers

2. pocket veto

3. 10 days

4. due process

---

1. 24th Amendment

2. preamble

3. suffrage

4. express powers

1. Money provided by the accused to ensure his appearance in court

2. The amendment that states the punishment must be appropriate to the crime committed

3. The amendment that grants 18-year-olds the right to vote

4. The first President to be affected by the amendment which ensures that there will always be a vice president

---

1. The amendment that guarantees the right to a trial by jury if the value of the disputed property exceeds $20

2. This amendment made citizens of former slaves and protected their rights.

3. This amendment was meant to punish the South for leaving the Union.

4. The minimum number of presidential electors for a state

---

1. The number of electors given to Washington, D.C., by the 23rd Amendment

2. It repealed Prohibition.

3. The legal term for going broke

4. Written letters of permission given to privateers allowing them to capture enemy ships and keep the cargo

---

1. Legal document that protects the rights of an owner's invention

2. The number of electors for a state with 23 representatives

3. Legal protection of ownership to those who write songs

4. The amendment that prohibits quartering soldiers in private homes

---

1. The constitutional amendment that gave the freed slaves the right to vote

2. The lame duck amendment

3. He is history's main source of information on the Constitution.

4. This amendment effectively canceled the three-fifths clause.

---

1. The amendment that prevents citizens of other states from suing a state in federal court

2. The President's role as head of the military

3. The President's annual message to the Congress and the people

4. The location of the "elastic clause"

---

1. The residence requirement for those seeking naturalization

2. The ceremony of installing the President in office

3. A law that singles out and punishes a person considered an undesirable

4. The secret to the Constitutional Convention's success (i.e., each side was willing to give in to its demands for the good of all)

---

1. Request to have an accused criminal returned to a state to face justice

2. The location of the national supremacy clause

3. The President's chief advisor on matters concerning America's public lands

4. The vote needed to approve the President's nomination of a foreign ambassador

1. 7th Amendment

2. 14th Amendment

3. 14th Amendment

4. 3

---

1. bail

2. 8th Amendment

3. 26th Amendment

4. Richard Nixon

---

1. patent

2. 25

3. copyright

4. 3rd Amendment

---

1. 3

2. 21st Amendment

3. bankruptcy

4. letters of marque

---

1. 11th Amendment

2. Commander in Chief

3. State of the Union message

4. Article 1, Section 8, clause 18

---

1. 15th Amendment

2. 20th Amendment

3. James Madison

4. 14th

---

1. extradition

2. Article 6

3. Secretary of Interior

4. simple majority of the Senate

---

1. 5 years

2. inauguration

3. bill of attainder

4. compromise

Answer Key

PAGE 11

1. b	2. d	3. a
4. a	5. c	6. b
7. d	8. a	9. e
10. a	11. a	12. b
13. c	14. e	15. a

PAGE 12

1. e	2. c	3. n
4. j	5. i	6. m
7. b	8. k	9. f
10. d	11. h	12. o
13. l	14. a	15. g

PAGE 13

1. The rights to continue living, to be free, and to pursue that which makes us happy so long as we do not violate the rights of others

2. The committee felt they would only get in each other's way if they tried to write it together. So they assigned Jefferson the task of drafting the document, indicating they would react when he was finished.

3. Whenever repeated violation of human rights and serious injustices are committed against the people; when the people have appealed to their government for a correction of their injustices without response

4. From the people

PAGE 14

5. Answers will vary.

6. That those who signed the Declaration would be marked men with the British. They needed to ally themselves together for their own protection.

7. He said he signed his name large enough so that King George would not have to use his bifocals to see it. The bold style in which he signed his name has become famous most probably because of the importance of the document he signed.

PAGE 21

1. Farmers were unhappy over farm prices and sought help from the national government. The government could offer no help because it had very little power. Other problems were caused by this same lack of power.

2. Weak central government, no power to tax, no power to regulate trade, no power to coin money and back it up with previous standard, no money to raise an army or navy, no federal court system, no power to enforce the laws it did make

PAGE 22

3. The larger states felt that since they had more people, they should have more representation in the lawmaking body (Virginia Plan). The smaller states feared being dominated and thus wanted equal representation in all states (New Jersey Plan). The Great Compromise—a Congress composed of both a house based on representation and a house where representation is equal.

4. Southern states wanted slaves counted as population when it came to determining representation, but they wanted to regard them as property for purposes of taxation to keep their state assessments lower. The three-fifths clause provided that three out of every five slaves would be counted in the population, both for determining representation and taxation.

PAGE 23

5. The basic framework and principles remain the same as they have for over 200 years. The changes (after the Bill of Rights) reflect social values that have changed through the years.

6. Answers will vary.

7. It feared the Convention would take away its power to tax goods that passed through the state.

PAGE 24

8. Almost all of the leaders of the day were men of note who had distinguished themselves through achievement. Financial success usually went along with the acclaim.

9. They figured there would be enough divisive issues that whatever compromises were eventually made would have a better chance of passing if the entire document were to be presented at one time in its final form.

Answer Key

1. F   2. T   3. T
4. T   5. F   6. T
7. T   8. F   9. T
10. F

PAGE 26

Answers will vary.

PAGE 27

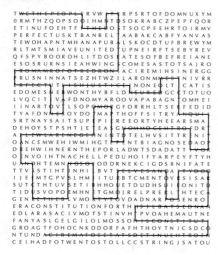

PAGE 34

1. Article 1 clearly outlines the legislative branch of our government.

2. The legislative department makes the laws.

3. House of Representatives and the U.S. Senate

4. Congress

5. House: 25 years old, 7 years, live in state, 2 years
   435 members
   Senate: 30 years old, 9 years, live in state, 6 years
   100 members

6. Speaker; answers will vary.

7. vice president; answers will vary.

PAGE 35

8. The number of people in the state; answers will vary.

9. The governor either calls for a special election or appoints someone to serve until the next general election.

10. The smaller states wanted equal representation; the larger states wanted representation based on population. The issue was finally decided by having both.

11. To provide a way to remove those in positions of trust who would misuse their power. As a check against abuses of power.

PAGE 36

12. The power was given to Congress to serve as a check in power on the other two branches of government—namely executive and judicial. The House stands as the accuser; the Senate conducts the trial.

13. simple majority; 2/3

14. Andrew Johnson and Bill Clinton

15. He was censured for attempting to fire one of Lincoln's cabinet members. Johnson was saved from conviction by one vote in the Senate.

16. Because the vice president, who would normally be presiding over the trial, would be next in line for the presidency should the president be convicted

17. He was accused in the Watergate scandal of ordering a break-in at Democratic headquarters to discover political plans and strategies. He resigned from office once the House Judiciary Committee made its recommendation to impeach him.

PAGE 37

18. Clinton was accused of inappropriate behavior with a White House intern, then denying it under oath when questioned by investigators. The lying under oath led to his impeachment but he was not convicted by the Senate.

19. Answers will vary.

20. Answers will vary.

Answer Key

PAGE 38

1. The Tuesday after the first Monday in November of all even numbered years

2. Answers will vary.

3. January 3

4. The secret ballot system ensures that voters can vote for whomever they choose without fear of harassment or discrimination.

5. simple majority; 218 in the House; 51 in the Senate

6. 2/3; 290; 67

7. Though it doesn't sound fair, the House members would probably have access to any evidence of wrongdoing against the candidate that the public might not have.

PAGE 39

8. 1/5

9. These men and women are the people we elected to make our laws. We have a right to know how they vote on laws that affect our interests and well-being. If we see they are not voting the way we like, we don't have to vote for them in the next election.

10. *Congressional Record*

11. 3 days

12. Both are required to pass legislation. The work of one house would be ineffective if the other was not in session.

13. Answer varies. They would have to answer to the people who pay their salaries—namely the taxpayers, the people who voted them into office.

14. In the days of Colonial America, King George's men would falsely detain those they considered threats on trumped-up charges, merely to keep them from causing trouble. The framers of the Constitution wanted its lawmakers to have the freedom to do what should be done.

15. It would be a position created while he was in office, thus he would be gaining from his own position as a congressman and this is forbidden in Article 1, Section 6, clause 2.

PAGE 40

Answers will vary.

PAGE 45

Answers will vary.

PAGE 46

1. Write or make phone calls to congresspersons, circulate petitions, publish views in newspapers

2. When the President is given legislation passed by Congress shortly before it adjourns, he may simply do nothing. If he doesn't have ten days while Congress is still in session to voice his objections, then his silence has the effect of a veto. Then the bill does not become a law. No.

3. The President is his party's leader, and a veto by him brings out a lot of party loyalty when an attempt is made to override his veto.

4. Some of the bills which have no effect on the public are allowed to become law without his signature simply to save time. This silence has the same effect as his signing the bills so long as Congress is in session.

5. To serve as a check against the power of Congress. The President's power would be greatly diminished if he did not have this capability. The influence of Congress would increase.

PAGE 50

1. 7	2. 8	3. 6
4. 2	5. 4	6. 1
7. 10	8. 15	9. 11
10. 13	11. 17	12. 9
13. 14	14. 16	15. 12
16. 3	17. 5	

PAGE 51

Answers will vary.

PAGE 52

1. Express powers are those specifically noted. Implied powers are the additional powers Congress was given to deal with matters that would emerge. Examples will vary, but the space program would be a good example.

2. Congress borrows money by issuing government bonds to the private sector.

3. A person must live in the U.S. for five years, pass a test on the U.S. Constitution plus other requirements.

4. Patents are issued to protect inventions. Copyrights protect books, songs, and other written material. The idea is to protect the genius of those who spend their time creating and to prevent others from profiting from their work.

Answer Key

1. A bill of attainder is a law directed at a specific individual. Ex post facto makes it against the law to have done something in the past that wasn't illegal at that time but later is. This paragraph was included because both were methods used by the British to quiet undesirables in Colonial America.

2. A writ of habeas corpus is a court order directing that an individual be brought before a court to determine if he or she is being jailed with probable good cause.

3. Guaranteeing until 1808 that slave trading would remain legal was a way of satisfying both slaveholders and those against slavery. In reality, it only delayed and intensified the confrontation.

4. Letters of marque were permissions to allow private citizens to capture enemy ships in exchange for the captured cargo, the idea being that intercepting supplies for the enemy would diminish its chance for success. However, the framers of the Constitution felt that it was like letting people take the law into their own hands and legalizing piracy.

5. There was a real bitterness toward England and its monarchy and a desire to throw off all remnants of the old and embrace democracy and equality.

6. The original Constitution stated that all direct taxes must be the same for everyone. The 16th Amendment provides for tax based on a person's wealth, which varies according to income.

PAGE 61

Crossword clues will vary.

1. Many of the people in the new nation could not read or write, and they were poorly informed of the affairs of the day because there was little media coverage, so a system giving the voting power to the more educated was created.

PAGE 62

2. The President was the man with the most electoral votes and the vice president was the runner-up. These two men were expected to work together. There would naturally be resentment by the vice president, and the two were more often than not political enemies. The President and vice president now run as a team on the same political ticket.

3. The President is a check against the power of Congress. He would always be trying to please them to get a pay raise and avoid a pay cut. Congress would also have the power to punish and reward a President, thus gaining too much control.

4. Answers will vary.

PAGE 64

1 f.	2. g	3. b
4. c	5. d	6. e
7. g	8. b	9. a/c
10. g	11. a	12. f
13. a/d	14. d/e	15. a

PAGE 65

Answers will vary.

PAGE 67

1. f	2. b	3. c
4. i	5. d	6. k
7. e	8. l	9. g
10. h	11. m	12. a
13. j	14. n	

Answer Key

PAGE 72

1. What is the main function of the Executive Department?
2. Who is the head of the executive branch of our government?
3. What is the President's title as the chief enforcer of the law?
4. What is the President's title as head of the armed forces?
5. What is the length of the President's term of office?
6. What is the title of the President's assistant?
7. What is the number of electors a state has?
8. When is Inauguration Day?
9. What are the qualifications for becoming President?
10. What do we call the President's group of chief advisors?
11. What vote is required to confirm treaties made by the President with foreign nations?
12. What is defined as betraying one's country?
13. Who actually elects the President?
14. How many members are in the President's cabinet?
15. What vote is required to confirm appointments made by the President?

PAGE 78

1. It is an attempt to divorce judges from any political association. Once chosen, the idea is to let them do what they are hired to do—make judicial decisions and not be concerned with the politics associated with being reelected.
2. Some stay on too long and become too old to do a good job. It's also difficult without an election to get rid of someone who doesn't do a good job.
3. impeachment, early retirement
4. a. appointment by the President
   b. confirmation by the Senate

PAGE 79

1. Answers will vary.
2. Answers will vary.

PAGE 80

1. a. appellate
   b. appellate
   c. original
2. a. U.S. District Court
   b. Supreme Court
   c. Circuit Court

PAGE 82

Judicial over Executive d, l
Judicial over Legislative d
Legislative over Judicial a, c, j, m
Legislative over Executive c, e, h, i, j
Executive over Judicial f, g
Executive over Legislative b, k

PAGE 83

1. legislative over executive
2. judicial over legislative, judicial over executive
3. legislative over judicial
4. executive over legislative, judicial over legislative
5. legislative over executive or executive over legislative
6. executive over legislative
7. executive over judicial

Answer Key

PAGE 84

1. Supreme
2. District
3. Circuit
4. President
5. Congress
6. original
7. appellate
8. judicial review
9. jury
10. 9
11. treason
12. 2
13. life
14. judge
15. simple majority, 5-4
16. unanimous, 12-0
17. impeachment by the House, conviction by the Senate
18. Chief Justice

PAGE 87

1. Each state had its own rules and tariffs to help its own citizens and discriminate against citizens of other states. The Constitution was designed to make each state recognize and value the rules and regulations of all other states.
2. Maine was split from Massachusetts in 1820. Virginia was divided into West Virginia and Virginia in 1863 following the outbreak of the Civil War.
3. In a true democracy, all the people make the rules. The size of the population would not make a true democracy possible in the United States.

PAGE 89

1. 27
2. 27 by Congress, 0 by special conventions
3. 26 by state legislatures, 1 by state conventions
4. 7 years
5. 38
6. There were many issues, but most centered around the controversy of the rights and status of women once they achieved equality. ERA never reached the necessary approval even though it was very close at times. Congress extended the deadline because of this.

PAGE 91

1. It was an announcement to the world that the U.S. would honor all debts accrued prior to the adoption of the Constitution.
2. The Constitution always rules. It points to the Constitution as the supreme law of the land rather than allowing the state to have rights that supersede federal laws.
3. They wanted a complete separation of church and state.

PAGE 93

1. 12
2. Rhode Island
3. 39
4. Pennsylvania
5. That it would have to be approved by nine of the twelve states who were represented at the Convention
6. Delaware
7. From September, 1787 until June, 1788. It went into effect in April, 1789.
8. A few states were hesitant to give up state rights; others had concerns about individual rights not being addressed.

Answer Key

PAGE 94

1. extradition
2. 9
3. Article 4
4. legislative
5. Maine and West Virginia
6. Congress
7. 39
8. September 17, 1787
9. 38
10. 27
11. Rhode Island
12. 2/3 of Congress, legislatures in 2/3 of the states call for a special convention
13. 3/4 of the state legislatures, conventions in 3/4 of the states
14. Congress
15. U.S. Constitution
16. 1789
17. republic
18. governor of the state

PAGE 102

1st Amendment

1. a. speech   b. press
   c. religion   d. petition
   e. assembly

2. If that which is said or written is not true but is presented as true or if it harms anyone unfairly.

3. A possible lawsuit in civil court for slander (oral statements) or for libel (written or printed statements)

4. If a practice of that religion is against the law or harmful to others

5. To assemble is to gather within a group to discuss issues. To petition is to circulate a written statement for the purpose of gaining signatures of those who are either for or against an issue.

2nd Amendment

6. That a person has a right to keep and bear arms to defend oneself

7. Gun registration laws; to keep guns out of the hands of criminals or mentally disturbed people

PAGE 103

3rd Amendment

8. Probably from the people of Boston, who were forced to house British military soldiers in their homes without permission

4th Amendment

9. A person's papers, home, possessions, person, or other "personal effects"

10. The date, the expected find, the location, a judge's signature, and the area to be searched

5th Amendment

11. A capital crime is a crime involving the death penalty as punishment. An infamous crime is a serious crime such as murder, robbery, or rape, as opposed to a misdemeanor, which is a minor crime.

12. A formal accusation charging the accused with a crime and ordering him or her to be bound over for trial

13. A grand jury examines the evidence against the accused to determine if there is enough damaging evidence against him to merit the case going to court.

14. 16-23, usually 23

15. The case goes to a petit jury to determine the guilt or innocence of the accused.

PAGE 104

16. That no person may be tried for the same crime more than once, assuming that he was acquitted the first time

17. That the defendant is not required to give testimony against himself which might lead to his conviction

18. The entire court's procedure, i.e., trial by jury, right to defense, etc.

6th Amendment

19. The trial shall take place in the state where the crime was committed.

20. So secret witnesses cannot bear witness against the accused

21. subpoena

7th Amendment

22. $20

23. a. where there was a question on a point of law

    b. where there has been a technical injustice in the court procedure

Answer Key

8th Amendment

24. Money provided to insure that the defendant will appear before the court on the appointed date

25. Pulling out fingernails, stocks, pillory, lopping off ears and hands, etc.

26. Answers will vary.

9th Amendment

27. Answers will vary.

28. It provides for implied rights, just as Article 1, Section 8 provides for implied power.

10th Amendment

29. They are reserved for the states and the people.

PAGE 106

1. 1st Amendment—People have the right to assemble peacefully to protest their government as long as they are not violent.

2. 4th Amendment—A warrant must contain exactly what the authorities expect to find.

3. 9th Amendment—One of the unlisted rights which an individual still has is the pursuit of happiness.

PAGE 107

4. 8th Amendment—The punishment must suit the crime.

5. 3rd Amendment—Quartering of soldiers in private homes is not allowed during peacetime and must be sanctioned by Congress during wartime.

6. 6th Amendment—He has the right to subpoena witnesses into court who have something to say on his behalf.

PAGE 108

7. 5th Amendment—A person acquitted of a crime cannot be tried again for the same crime.

8. 2nd Amendment—Kiana needs a permit to carry a loaded weapon, even if it is for her own self-defense.

9. 7th Amendment—Both parties have a right to a trial by jury.

10. 10th Amendment—The state has the right to regulate its education system.

PAGE 113

1. Pros: Conflict of ideas and values should keep both on their toes and provide for an honest government. Cons: Constant quarreling and a lack of political harmony.

2. It became clear that there would be many more ties because giving each elector two votes would result in his party loyalty dictating that he vote for both his party's candidates.

3. The two ended up in a pistol duel in which Burr killed Hamilton.

4. Answers will vary.

PAGE 114

1. That they cannot be heard in federal courts

2. They thought it gave the federal courts too much power.

3.

As Defined in Article 2	Under the 12th Amendment
the Electoral College	the Electoral College
the state legislators	the people
a majority of electors	a majority of electors
the candidate with the second greatest number of electoral votes	Each party runs two candidates—one for president and one for vice president. The party that wins the most electors gets both the president and vice president.

PAGE 116

1. Answers will vary.

2. 538

3. 270

4. Because of the winner-take-all philosophy, it is important to win as many of the big states as possible.

5. Answers will vary according to most recent census and reassignment of electors.

6. Every state has two U.S. senators and at least one representative.

Answer Key

PAGE 121

1. To officially abolish slavery

2. Anyone born or naturalized as a citizen has the same rights as all citizens.

3. To give African Americans a greater status in society—to upgrade them to the level of American citizenship and to reverse the Dred Scott decision

4. No longer can African Americans be counted as three-fifths. Every person is counted.

5. 21 years old, male inhabitant, citizen of the United States, can't have participated in crimes against the United States

6. The state's representation in the House shall be cut proportionally.

7. 2/3

PAGE 122

8. The South could not pay any of its war debts, and the North's debts would all be honored and paid in full.

9. To protect the voting rights of minority groups.

10. To include not only African Americans but also other minorities

11. poll taxes, literacy tests

PAGE 123

Answers will vary.

PAGE 124

1. Prior to the 17th Amendment, they were chosen by the state legislature. Now they are elected by the people.

2. The governor can call for a special election, or the governor appoints someone to serve until the next general election when someone will be elected to finish the unexpired term.

PAGE 125

1. 1919

2. The Volstead Act, introduced by Andrew J. Volstead of Minnesota, enforced the 18th Amendment.

PAGE 131

1. once each year

2. Prior to the amendment, it was November to March 4; now it's from November to January 20 for the President. Prior to the amendment it was November until the next December; now it's from November to January 3 for Congress.

3. Congress will decide.

4. It's an ineffective time when the old Congress and President are pretty much without power.

5. January 20

6. January 3

PAGE 133

1. Americans had no desire to be told what to do. World War I had just ended and people felt it was time to have fun. Also there weren't enough federal agents to enforce the mechanics of the Volstead Act.

2. Members of Congress felt since public pressure had brought about the 18th Amendment, and public pressure was bringing an end to Prohibition, the people themselves ought to have a hand in the final decision. So they chose the convention method where private individuals would be chosen as delegates.

3. It is against Communism, monopoly, gambling, pornography, drugs, and socialized medicine.

PAGE 135

1. Franklin D. Roosevelt was elected President four times. Many people felt that was too long for one person to serve as President.

2. Dwight D. Eisenhower

3. He could serve up to two years of another elected President's term; then he could be elected to the office twice himself.

4. Yes, he could run in 1976 and did, but he lost to Jimmy Carter. If he had been elected in 1976, he could not have run in 1980 because the combined time would have given him longer than ten years as President.

5. Answers will vary.

Answer Key

PAGE 136

1. It has the same number as the smallest state. The least number a state can have is three (every state has two senators and at least one representative).

2. 538

3. 270

PAGE 137

1. A tax to vote

2. Mainly to discriminate

3. In most state elections, national officials would be elected at the same time, and the state would have to print two separate ballots.

PAGE 140

1. In 1973, Vice President Spiro Agnew resigned. President Nixon appointed Gerald Ford as vice president. In August of 1974, Nixon resigned as President and Gerald Ford became President. Ford then chose Nelson Rockefeller to serve as his vice president.

2. He or she must have agreement from a majority of the cabinet and 2/3 of both houses of Congress.

3. He merely notifies the leaders of both houses of Congress.

4. His doctor would be the best judge.

PAGE 141

1. Answers will vary but should include proof of citizenship.

2. Answers will vary.

PAGE 142

1. Article I, Section 6, clause 1 gave the members of Congress the power to establish their own compensation. It seems only fair that once they vote themselves a pay raise, they should face the test of an election before they start receiving the new salary.

2. This issue has long been a point of contention among many Americans. The pressure they brought to bear finally brought the change to a reality.

3. Since only one third of the members are elected every two years, logic would dictate that the change would follow the election of Representatives.

4. Answers may vary over time.

PAGE 143

1. 4	2. 9	3. 15
4. 17	5. 19	6. 6
7. 1	8. 7	

PAGE 144

9. 12	10. 14	11. 24
12. 20	13. 5	14. 2
15. 3	16. 27	17. 16

PAGE 145

18. 26	19. 23	20. 11
21. 22	22. 18	23. 21
24. 25	25. 8	26. 13
27. 10		

PAGE 146

1. Article 1, Section 8, clause 3. Congress can control trade.

2. Article 1, Section 2, clause 1. House members are chosen every two years.

3. Article 1, Section 7, clause 3. Congress needs approval by the President on all matters except impeachment and adjournment.

4. 6th Amendment. The accused has the right to be confronted with witnesses against him.

5. Article 3, Section 1. Federal judges serve for life.

6. Article 2, Section 2, clause 2. Simple majority of the Senate.

Answer Key

PAGE 147

7. 25th Amendment, Section 4. If a majority of the cabinet agrees that the President is unable to return, it notifies Congress. It takes 2/3 of each house to keep him out.

8. Article 2, Section 1, clause 5. The minimum age for a President is 35 years old.

9. Article 2, Section 1, clause 3 or 12th Amendment. In such case, the President is elected by the House of Representatives.

10. Article 4, Section 2, clause 2. A fleeing criminal can be apprehended and returned to the state where he is accused on demand of the governor.

11. Article 2, Section 2, clause 1. The President shall be Commander in Chief of the armed forces.

12. 2nd Amendment. The right of the people to keep and bear arms shall not be infringed.

13. Article 1, Section 2, clause 4. The House of Representatives shall have the sole power of impeachment.

PAGE 148

14. 22nd Amendment. No President may be elected more than twice nor serve more than ten years.

15. 8th Amendment. Excessive bail and fines are not allowed.

16. Article 3, Section 3, clause 1. No person shall be convicted of treason without the testimony of two eyewitnesses or an open confession.

17. Article 4, Section 3, clause 1. New states may be admitted into the Union by Congress.

18. Article 5. Three-fourths of the state legislatures are required to ratify amendments.

19. 5th Amendment. The right of eminent domain gives the government the right to take land of private individuals for the good of all, but a just price must be paid.

20. Article 1, Section 10, clause 1. No state may coin money.

076822456X • Our Living Constitution

Notes